OPERATING SYSTEMS

CONCEPTS

G. SREEHITHA REDDY
K. REDDY PRADEEP

INDIA · SINGAPORE · MALAYSIA

Notion Press

Old No. 38, New No. 6
McNichols Road, Chetpet
Chennai - 600 031

First Published by Notion Press 2019
Copyright © G. Sreehitha Reddy, K. Reddy Pradeep 2019
All Rights Reserved.

ISBN 978-1-64678-981-8

Dedication

To My Family for their Motivation and Encouragement and my daughter

– Mrs. G. Sreehitha Reddy

To My Parents, Wife and Daughter (Khasvi) for their Love and Support

– Mr. K. Reddy Pradeep

Contents

Unit I. Operating System

Unit II.   Process Management

Unit III.   Deadlock

Unit IV.   Memory Management

Unit V.   File System

Unit VI.   I/O Systems

Preface

This book is an introduction to Operating Systems for Undergraduates. In this course, you will familiarize yourself with the basic concepts of Operating Systems. An operating system (OS) is a collection of software that manages computer hardware resources and provides common services for computer programs. The operating system is a vital component of the system software in a computer system. Application programs usually require an operating system to function. We will go over the Overview of OS, Process Management, Memory Management, Files, I/O Systems, Protection and Security. We hope the practitioners will find it useful. As prerequisites, we assume reader is clear with the basic data structures, computer organization, C.

The intent of this book is to provide a thorough discussion of the fundamentals of operating system design and to relate these to contemporary design issues and to current directions in the development of operating systems. Operating Systems concepts are presented in a descriptive manner. Formula proofs are largely omitted. The fundamental concepts and algorithms covered are often based on both commercial and open source operating system. The book is intended for both academic and professional audience. As a text book, it is intended as a one semester undergraduate course in operating system for computer science, computer engineering and electrical engineering majors. It covers all the core topics and most of the elective topics.

Acknowledgements

We would like to thank who have provided invaluable feedback on the textbook. The result, we hope, is greater clarity for readers. We would also like to acknowledge the contributions, influence, and support of the following people. We have included organization affiliation if we could figure it out.

Dr. A. Rama Mohan Reddy	Professor, S.V University, Tirupati, India
Dr. D. Vivekananda Reddy	Assistant professor, S.V University, Tirupati, India
Dr. K. Sekar	Vice Principal, SVCE, Tirupati, India
Dr. B. Ramasubba Reddy	Vice Principal, SVEC, Tirupati, India
Mr. Suresh Avula	Design Engineer, Adtran, Huntsville.

Our gratitude towards the following dearest persons.

Mr. G. Rama Murthy Reddy & Mrs. N. Bhoodevi

Mr. K. Kodanda Ram & Mrs. K. Uma Maheswari

Mr. G. Srikar	Senior Android Engineer, Finbox, Banglore, India.
Mr. K. Reddy Sandeep	Application Support Engineer, Clover Infotech, Banglore, India.

Finally, our special thanks to our well wishers for their encouragement.

Operating System

Introduction

- An operating system is a program which manages all the computer hardware.
- It provides the base for application program and acts as an intermediary between a user and the computer hardware.
- The operating system has two objectives such as:

  - Firstly, an operating system controls the computer's hardware.
  - The second objective is to provide an interactive interface to the user and interpret commands so that it can communicate with the hardware.

- The operating system is very important part of almost every computer system.

Managing Hardware

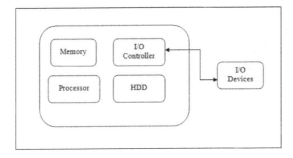

- The prime objective of operating system is to manage & control the various hardware resources of a computer system.
- These hardware resources include processer, memory, and disk space and so on.
- The output result was display in monitor. In addition to communicating with the hardware theoperating system provides on error handling procedure and display an error notification.

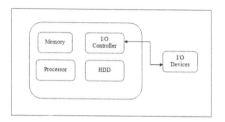

- If a device not functioning properly, the operating system cannot be communicate with the device.

Providing an Interface

- The operating system organizes application so that users can easily access, use and store them.
- It provides a stable and consistent way for applications to deal with the hardware without the user having known details of the hardware.
- If the program is not functioning properly, the operating system again takes control, stops the application and displays the appropriate error message.
- Computer system components are divided into 5 parts

  - Computer hardware
  - Operating system
  - Utilities
  - Application programs
  - End User

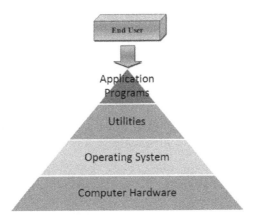

- The operating system controls and coordinate a user of hardware and various application programs for various users.
- It is a program that directly interacts with the hardware.
- The operating system is the first encoded with the Computer and it remains on the memory all time thereafter.

System Goals

- The purpose of an operating system is to be provided an environment in which an user can execute programs.
- Its primary goals are to make the computer system convenience for the user.
- Its secondary goals are to use the computer hardware in efficient manner.

View of Operating System

- **User view:** The user view of the computer varies by the interface being used. The examples are – windows XP, vista, windows 7 etc. Most computer user sit in the in front of personal computer (pc) in this case the operating system is designed mostly for easy use with some attention paid to resource utilization. Some user sit at a terminal connected to a mainframe/minicomputer. In this case other users are accessing the same computer through the other terminals. There user are share resources and may exchange the information. The operating system in this case is designed to maximize resources utilization to assume that all available CPU time, memory and I/O are used efficiently and no individual user takes more than his/her fair and share.The other users sit at workstations connected to network of other workstations and servers. These users have dedicated resources but they share resources such as networking and servers like file, compute and print server. Here the operating system is designed to compromise between individual usability and resource utilization.

- **System view:** From the computer point of view the operating system is the program which is most intermediate with the hardware. An operating system has resources as hardware and software which may be required to solve a problem like CPU time, memory space, file storage space and I/O devices and so on. That's why the operating system acts as manager of these resources. Another view of the operating system is it is a control program. A control program manages the execution of user programs to present the errors in proper use of the computer. It is especially concerned of the user the operation and controls the I/O devices.

Types of Operating System

1. **Mainframe System:** It is the system where the first computer used to handle many commercial scientific applications. The growth of mainframe systems traced from simple batch system where the computer runs one and only one application to time shared systems which allowed for user interaction with the computer system

a. **Batch /Early System:** Early computers were physically large machine. The common input devices were card readers, tape drivers. The common output devices were line printers, tape drivers and card punches. In these systems the user did not interact directly with the computer system. Instead the user preparing a job which consists of programming data and some control information and then submitted it to the computer operator after some time the output is appeared. The output in these early computer was fairly simple is main task was to transfer control automatically from one job to next. The operating system always resides in the memory. To speed up processing operators batched the jobs with similar needs and ran then together as a group. The disadvantages of batch system are that in this execution environment the CPU is often idle because the speed up of I/O devices is much slower than the CPU.

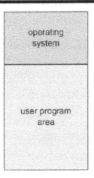

Memory Layout for a Simple Batch System

b. **Multiprogrammed System:** Multiprogramming concept increases CPU utilization by organization jobs so that the CPU always has one job to execute the idea behind multiprogramming concept. The operating system keeps several jobs in memory simultaneously as shown in below figure.

Operating System
Job 1
Job 2
Job 3
Job 4

This set of job is subset of the jobs kept in the job pool. The operating system picks and beginning to execute one of the jobs in the memory. In this environment the operating system simply switches and executes another job. When a job needs to wait the CPU is simply switched to another job and so on. The multiprogramming operating system is sophisticated because the operating system makes decisions for the user. This is known as scheduling. If several jobs are ready to run at the same time the system choose one among them. This is known as CPU scheduling. The disadvantages of the multiprogrammed system are

- It does not provide user interaction with the computer system during the program execution.
- The introduction of disk technology solved these problems rather than reading the cards from card reader into disk. This form of processing is known as spooling.

SPOOL stands for simultaneous peripheral operations online. It uses the disk as a huge buffer for reading from input devices and for storing output data until the output devices accept them. It is also use for processing data at remote sides. The remote processing is done and its own speed with no CPU intervention. Spooling overlaps the input, output one job with computation of other jobs.

Spooling has a beneficial effect on the performance of the systems by keeping both CPU and I/O devices working at much higher time.

c. **Time Sharing System:**The time sharing system is also known as multi user systems. The CPU executes multiple jobs by switching among them but the switches occurs so frequently that the user can interact with each program while it is running. An interactive computer system provides direct communication between a user and system. The user gives instruction to the operating systems or to a program directly using keyboard or mouse and wait for immediate results. So the response time will be short. The time sharing system allows many users to share the computer simultaneously. Since each action in this system is short, only a little CPU time is needed for each user. The system switches rapidly from one user to the next so each user feels as if the entire computer system is dedicated to his use, even though it is being shared by many users. The disadvantages of time sharing system are:

- ⋏ It is more complex than multiprogrammed operating system
- ⋏ The system must have memory management & protection, since several jobs are kept in memory at the same time.
- ⋏ Time sharing system must also provide a file system, so disk management is required.
- ⋏ It provides mechanism for concurrent execution which requires complex CPU scheduling schemes.

2. **Personal Computer System/Desktop System:** Personal computer appeared in 1970's. They are microcomputers that are smaller & less expensive than mainframe systems. Instead of maximizing CPU & peripheral utilization, the systems opt

for maximizing user convenience & responsiveness. At first file protection was not necessary on a personal machine. But when other computers 2nd other users can access the files on a pc file protection becomes necessary. The lack of protection made if easy for malicious programs to destroy data on such systems. These programs may be self replicating& they spread via worm or virus mechanisms. They can disrupt entire companies or even world wide networks. E.g: windows 98, windows 2000, Linux.

3. **Microprocessor Systems/ Parallel Systems/ Tightly coupled Systems:** These Systems have more than one processor in close communications which share the computer bus, clock, memory & peripheral devices. Ex: UNIX, LINUX. Multiprocessor Systems have 3 main advantages.

   a. **Increased throughput:** No. of processes computed per unit time. By increasing the no. of processors move work can be done in less time. The speed up ratio with N processors is not N, but it is less than N. Because a certain amount of overhead is incurred in keeping all the parts working correctly.

   b. **Increased Reliability:** If functions can be properly distributed among several processors, then the failure of one processor will not halt the system, but slow it down. This ability to continue to operate in spite of failure makes the system fault tolerant.

   c. **Economic scale:** Multiprocessor systems can save money as they can share peripherals, storage & power supplies.

   The various types of multiprocessing systems are:

   ↗ **Symmetric Multiprocessing (SMP):** Each processor runs an identical copy of the operating system & these copies communicate with one another as required.

Ex: Encore's version of UNIX for multi max computer. Virtually, all modern operating system including Windows NT, Solaris, Digital UNIX, OS/2 & LINUX now provide support for SMP.

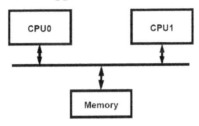

A **Asymmetric Multiprocessing (Master – Slave Processors):** Each processor is designed for a specific task. A master processor controls the system & schedules & allocates the work to the slave processors. Ex – Sun's Operating system SUNOS version 4 provides asymmetric multiprocessing.

4. **Distributed System/Loosely Coupled Systems:** In contrast to tightly coupled systems, the processors do not share memory or a clock. Instead, each processor has its own local memory. The processors communicate with each other by various communication lines such as high speed buses or telephone lines. Distributed systems depend on networking for their functionalities. By being able to communicate distributed systems are able to share computational tasks and provide a rich set of features to the users. Networks vary by the protocols used, the distances between the nodes and transport media. TCP/IP is the most common network protocol. The processor is a distributed system varies in size and function. It may microprocessors, work stations, minicomputer, and large general purpose computers. Network types are based on the distance between the nodes such as LAN (within a room, floor or building) and WAN (between buildings, cities or countries).

The advantages of distributed system are resource sharing, computation speed up, reliability, communication.

5. **Real time Systems:** Real time system is used when there are rigid time requirements on the operation of a processor or flow of data. Sensors bring data to the computers. The computer analyzes data and adjusts controls to modify the sensors inputs. System that controls scientific experiments, medical imaging systems and some display systems are real time systems. The disadvantages of real time system are:

   a. A real time system is considered to function correctly only if it returns the correct result within the time constraints.
   b. Secondary storage is limited or missing instead data is usually stored in short term memory or ROM.
   c. Advanced OS features are absent.
      Real time system is of two types such as:

      ⋏ **Hard real time systems:** It guarantees that the critical task has been completed on time. The sudden task is takes place at a sudden instant of time.
      ⋏ **Soft real time systems:** It is a less restrictive type of real time system where a critical task gets priority over other tasks and retains that priority until it computes. These have more limited utility than hard real time systems. Missing an occasional deadline is acceptable e.g. QNX, VX works. Digital audio or multimedia is included in this category.

It is a special purpose OS in which there are rigid time requirements on the operation of a processor. A real time OS has well defined fixed time constraints. Processing must be done within the time constraint or the system will fail. A real time system is said to function correctly only if it returns the correct result within the time constraint. These systems are characterized by having time as a key parameter.

Basic Functions of Operation System

The various functions of operating system are as follows:

1. Process Management

A program does nothing unless their instructions are executed by a CPU.A process is a program in execution. A time shared user program such as a complier is a process. A word processing program being run by an individual user on a pc is a process.

- A system task such as sending output to a printer is also a process. A process needs certain resources including CPU time, memory files & I/O devices to accomplish its task.
- These resources are either given to the process when it is created or allocated to it while it is running. The OS is responsible for the following activities of process management.
- Creating & deleting both user & system processes.
- Suspending & resuming processes.
- Providing mechanism for process synchronization.
- Providing mechanism for process communication.
- Providing mechanism for deadlock handling.

2. Main Memory Management

The main memory is central to the operation of a modern computer system. Main memory is a large array of words or bytes ranging in size from hundreds of thousand to billions. Main memory stores the quickly accessible data shared by the CPU & I/O device. The central processor reads instruction from main memory during instruction fetch cycle & it both reads &writes data from main memory during the data fetch cycle. The main memory is generally the only large storage device that the CPU is able to address & access directly. For example, for the CPU to process data from disk. Those data must first be transferred to main memory by CPU generated E/O calls. Instruction must be in memory for the CPU to execute them. The OS is responsible for the following activities in connection with memory management.

- Keeping track of which parts of memory are currently being used & by whom.
- Deciding which processes are to be loaded into memory when memory space becomes available.
- Allocating &deallocating memory space as needed.

3. File Management

File management is one of the most important components of an OS computer can store information on several different types of physical media magnetic tape, magnetic disk & optical disk are the most common media. Each medium is controlled by a device such as disk drive or tape drive those has unique characteristics. These characteristics include access speed, capacity, data transfer rate & access method (sequential or random).For convenient use of computer system the OS provides a uniform logical view of information storage. The OS abstracts from the physical properties of its storage devices to define a logical storage unit the file. A file is collection of related information defined by its creator. The OS is responsible for the following activities of file management.

- Creating & deleting files.
- Creating & deleting directories.
- Supporting primitives for manipulating files & directories.
- Mapping files into secondary storage.
- Backing up files on non-volatile media.

4. I/O System Management

One of the purposes of an OS is to hide the peculiarities of specific hardware devices from the user. For example, in UNIX the peculiarities of I/O devices are hidden from the bulk of the OS itself by the I/O subsystem. The I/O subsystem consists of:

- A memory management component that includes buffering, catching & spooling.
- A general device – driver interfaces drivers for specific hardware devices. Only the device driver knows the peculiarities of the specific device to which it is assigned.

5. Secondary Storage Management

The main purpose of computer system is to execute programs. These programs with the data they access must be in main memory during execution. As the main memory is too small to accommodate all data & programs & because the data that it holds are lost when power is lost. The computer system must provide secondary storage to back-up main memory. Most modern computer systems are disks as the storage medium to store data & program. The operating system is responsible for the following activities of disk management.

- Free space management.
- Storage allocation.
- Disk scheduling

Because secondary storage is used frequently it must be used efficiently.

Networking

A distributed system is a collection of processors that don't share memory peripheral devices or a clock. Each processor has its own local memory & clock and the processor communicate with one another through various communication lines such as high speed buses or networks. The processors in the system are connected through communication networks which are configured in a number of different ways. The communication network design must consider message routing & connection strategies are the problems of connection & security.

Protection or security

If a computer system has multi users & allow the concurrent execution of multiple processes then the various processes must be protected from one another's activities. For that purpose, mechanisms ensure that files, memory segments, CPU & other resources can be operated on by only those processes that have gained proper authorization from the OS.

Command Interpretation

One of the most important functions of the OS is connected interpretation where it acts as the interface between the user & the OS.

System Calls

System calls provide the interface between a process & the OS. These are usually available in the form of assembly language instruction. Some systems allow system calls to be made directly from a high level language program like C, BCPL and PERL etc. systems calls occur in different ways depending on the computer in use. System calls can be roughly grouped into 5 major categories.

1. Process Control

- **End, abort:** A running program needs to be able to has its execution either normally (end) or abnormally (abort).
- **Load, execute:** A process or job executing one program may want to load and executes another program.
- **Create Process, terminate process:** There is a system call specifying for the purpose of creating a new process or job (create process or submit job). We may want to terminate a job or process that we created (terminates process, if we find that it is incorrect or no longer needed).
- **Get process attributes, set process attributes:** If we create a new job or process we should able to control its execution. This control requires the ability to determine & reset the attributes of a job or processes (get process attributes, set process attributes).
- **Wait time:** After creating new jobs or processes, we may need to wait for them to finish their execution (wait time).
- **Wait event, signal event:** We may wait for a specific event to occur (wait event). The jobs or processes then signal when that event has occurred (signal event).

2. File Manipulation

- **Create file, delete file:** We first need to be able to create & delete files. Both the system calls require the name of the file & some of its attributes.
- **Open file, close file:** Once the file is created, we need to open it & use it. We close the file when we are no longer using it.
- **Read, write, reposition file:** After opening, we may also read, write or reposition the file (rewind or skip to the end of the file).
- **Get file attributes, set file attributes:** For either files or directories, we need to be able to determine the values of various attributes & reset them if necessary. Two system calls get file attribute & set file attributes are required for their purpose.

3. Device Management

- **Request device, release device:** If there are multiple users of the system, we first request the device. After we finished with the device, we must release it.
- **Read, write, reposition:** Once the device has been requested & allocated to us, we can read, write & reposition the device.

4. Information maintenance

- **Get time or date, set time or date:**Most systems have a system call to return the current date & time or set the current date & time.
- **Get system data, set system data:** Other system calls may return information about the system like number of current users, version number of OS, amount of free memory etc.
- **Get process attributes, set process attributes:** The OS keeps information about all its processes & there are system calls to access this information.

5. Communication

There are two modes of communication such as:

- **Message passing model:** Information is exchanged through an inter process communication facility provided by operating system. Each computer in a network has a name by which it is known. Similarly, each process has a process name which is translated to an equivalent identifier by which the OS can refer to it. The get hostid and get processed systems calls to do this translation. These identifiers are then passed to the general purpose open & close calls provided by the file system or to specific open connection system call. The recipient process must give its permission for communication to take place with an accept connection call. The source of the communication known as client & receiver known as server exchange messages by read message & write message system calls. The close connection call terminates the connection.

- **Shared memory model:** processes use map memory system calls to access regions of memory owned by other processes. They exchange information by reading & writing data in the shared areas. The processes ensure that they are not writing to the same location simultaneously.

System Programs

System programs provide a convenient environment for program development & execution. They are divided into the following categories.

- **File manipulation:** These programs create, delete, copy, rename, print & manipulate files and directories.
- **Status information:** Some programs ask the system for date, time & amount of available memory or disk space, no. of users or similar status information.
- **File modification:**Several text editors are available to create and modify the contents of file stored on disk.
- **Programming language support:** compliers, assemblers & interpreters are provided to the user with the OS.
- **Programming loading and execution:** Once a program is assembled or compiled, it must be loaded into memory to be executed.
- **Communications:** These programs provide the mechanism for creating virtual connections among processes users 2nd different computer systems.
- **Application programs:** Most OS are supplied with programs that are useful to solve common problems or perform common operations. Ex: web browsers, word processors & text formatters etc.

System Structure

1. **Simple structure:** There are several commercial system that don't have a well – defined structure such operating systems begins as small, simple & limited systems and then grow beyond their original scope. MS-DOS is an example of such system. It was not divided into modules carefully. Another example of limited structuring is the UNIX operating system.

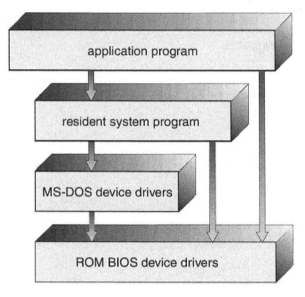

(MS DOS Structure)

2. **Layered approach:** In the layered approach, the OS is broken into a number of layers (levels) each built on top of lower layers. The bottom layer (layer o) is the hardware & top most layer (layer N) is the user interface. The main advantage of the layered approach is modularity.

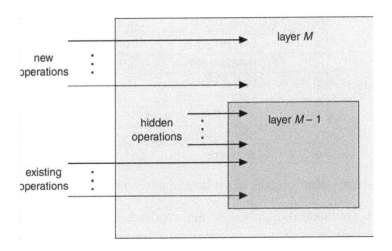

▲ The layers are selected such that each users functions (or operations) & services of only lower layer.

▲ This approach simplifies debugging & system verification, i.e. the first layer can be debugged without concerning the rest of the system. Once the first layer is debugged, its correct functioning is assumed while the 2nd layer is debugged & so on.

▲ If an error is found during the debugging of a particular layer, the error must be on that layer because the layers below it are already debugged. Thus the design & implementation of the system are simplified when the system is broken down into layers.

▲ Each layer is implemented using only operations provided by lower layers. A layer doesn't need to know how these operations are implemented; it only needs to know what these operations do.

▲ The layer approach was first used in the operating system. It was defined in six layers.

Layers	Functions
5	User Program
4	I/O Management
3	Operator Process Communication
2	Memory Management
1	CPU Scheduling
0	Hardware

The main disadvantage of the layered approach is:

- The main difficulty with this approach involves the careful definition of the layers, because a layer can use only those layers below it. For example, the device driver for the disk space used by virtual memory algorithm must be at a level lower than that of the memory management routines, because memory management requires the ability to use the disk space.
- It is less efficient than a non layered system (Each layer adds overhead to the system call & the net result is a system call that take longer time than on a non layered system).

Virtual Machines

By using CPU scheduling & virtual memory techniques an operating system can create the illusion of multiple processes, each executing on its own processors & own virtual memory. Each processor is provided a virtual copy of the underlying computer. The resources of the computer are shared to create the virtual machines. CPU scheduling can be used to create the appearance that users have their own processor.

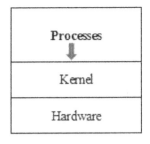

Processes
⬇
Kernel
Hardware

Process	Process	Process
⬇	⬇	⬇
Kernel	Kernel	Kernel
Virtual Machine Hardware		

(Non virtual Machine)   (Virtual Machine)

Implementation: Although the virtual machine concept is useful, it is difficult to implement since much effort is required to provide an exact duplicate of the underlying machine. The CPU is being multi-programmed among several virtual machines, which slows down the virtual machines in various ways.

Difficulty: A major difficulty with this approach is regarding the disk system. The solution is to provide virtual disks, which are identical in all respects except size. These are known as mini disks in IBM's VM OS. The sum of sizes of all mini disks should be less than the actual amount of physical disk space available.

I/O Structure

A general purpose computer system consists of a CPU and multiple device controller which is connected through a common bus. Each device controller is in charge of a specific type of device. A device controller maintains some buffer storage and a set of special purpose register. The device controller is responsible for moving the data between peripheral devices and buffer storage.

I/O Interrupt: To start an I/O operation the CPU loads the appropriate register within the device controller. In turn the device controller examines the content of the register to determine the actions which will be taken. For example, suppose the device controller finds the read request then, the controller will start the transfer of data from the device to the buffer. Once the transfer of data is complete the device controller informs the CPU that the operation has been finished. Once the I/O is started, two actions are possible such as

- In the simplest case the I/O is started then at I/O completion control is return to the user process. This is known as synchronous I/O.

- The other possibility is asynchronous I/O in which the control is return to the user program without waiting for the I/O completion. The I/O then continues with other operations.

When an interrupt occurs first determine which I/O device is responsible for interrupting. After searching the I/O device table the signal goes to the each I/O request. If there are additional request waiting in the queue for one device the operating system starts processing the next request.

Finally control is return from the I/O interrupt.

DMA controller: DMA is used for high speed I/O devices. In DMA access the device controller transfers on entire block of data to of from its own buffer storage to memory. In this access the interrupt is generated per block rather than one interrupt per byte. The operating system finds a buffer from the pool of buffers for the transfer. Then a portion of the operating system called a device driver sets the DMA controller registers to use appropriate source and destination addresses and transfer length. The DMA controller is then instructed to start the I/O operation. While the DMA controller is performing the data transfer, the CPU is free to perform other tasks. Since the memory generally can transfer only one word at a time, the DMA controller steals memory cycles from the CPU. This cycle stealing can slow down the CPU execution while a DMA transfer is in progress. The DMA controller interrupts the CPU when the transfer has been completed.

Storage Structure

The storage structure of a computer system consists of two types of memory such as

- Main memory
- Secondary memory

Basically the programs & data are resided in main memory during the execution. The programs and data are not stored permanently due to following two reasons.

- Main memory is too small to store all needed programs and data permanently.
- Main memory is a volatile storage device which lost its contents when power is turned off. **Main Memory:**The main memory and the registers are the only storage area that the CPU can access the data directly without any help of other device. The machine instruction which take memory address as arguments do not take disk address. Therefore in execution any instructions and any data must be resided in any one of direct access storage device. If the data are not in memory they must be moved before the CPU can operate on them. There are two types of main memory such as:

RAM (Random Access Memory): The RAM is implemented in a semiconductor technology is called D-RAM (Dynamic RAM) which forms an array of memory words/cells. Each & every word should have its own address/locator. Instruction is performed through a sequence of load and store instruction to specific memory address. Each I/O controller includes register to hold commands of the data being transferred. To allow more convenient access to I/O device many computer architecture provide memory mapped I/O. In the case of memory mapped I/O ranges of memory address are mapped to the device register. Read and write to this memory addressbecause the data to be transferred to and from the device register.

Secondary Storage: The most common secondary storage devices are magnetic disk and magnetic tape which provide permanent storage of programs and data.

Magnetic Disk: It provides the bulk of secondary storage for modern computer systems. Each disk platter has flat circular shape like a CD. The diameter of a platter range starts from 1.8 to 5.25 inches. The two surfaces of a platter are covered with a magnetic material which records the information/data is given by the user. The read, write head are attached to a disk arm, which moves all the heads as a unit. The surface of a platter is logically divided into circular tracks which are sub divided into sectors. The set of tracks which are at one arm position forms a cylinder. There are may be thousands of cylinders in a disk drive & each track contains 100 of sectors. The storage capacity of a common disk drive is measured in GB. When the disk is in use a drive motor spins it at high speed. Most drives rotated 62 to 200 time/sec. The disk speed has two parts such as transfer rate & positioning time. The transfer rate is the rate at which data flow between the drive & the computer. The positioning time otherwise called as random access time. It consists of two parts such as seek time & rotational latency. The seek time is the time taken to move the disk arc to the desired cylinder. The rotational latency is the time taken to rotate the disk head.

Magnetic Tape: It was used as early secondary storage medium. It is also permanent and can hold large quantity of data. Its access time is slower, comparison to main memory devices. Magnetic tapes are sequential in nature. That's why random access to magnetic tape is thousand times slower than the random access to magnetic disk. The magnetic tapes are used mainly for backup the data. The magnetic tape must be kept in a non dusty environment and temperature controlled area. But the main advantage of the secondary storage device is that it can hold 2 to 3 times more data than a large disk drive. There are 4 types of magnetic tapes such as:

- ½ Inch
- ¼ Inch
- 4 mm
- 8 mm

Operating System Services

An operating system provides an environment for the execution of the program. It provides some services to the programs. The various services provided by an operating system are as follows:

- **Program Execution:** The system must be able to load a program into memory and to run that program. The program must be able to terminate this execution either normally or abnormally.
- **I/O Operation:** A running program may require I/O. This I/O may involve a file or a I/O device for specific device. Some special function can be desired. Therefore the operating system must provide a means to do I/O.
- **File System Manipulation:** The programs need to create and delete files by name and read and write files. Therefore the operating system must maintain each and every files correctly.

- **Communication:** The communication is implemented via shared memory or by the technique of message passing in which packets of information are moved between the processes by the operating system.
- **Error detection:** The operating system should take the appropriate actions for the occurrences of any type like arithmetic overflow, access to the illegal memory location and too large user CPU time.
- **Research Allocation:** When multiple users are logged on to the system the resources must be allocated to each of them. For current distribution of the resource among the various processes the operating system uses the CPU scheduling run times which determine which process will be allocated with the resource.
- **Accounting:** The operating system keep track of which users use how many and which kind of computer resources.
- **Protection:** The operating system is responsible for both hardware as well as software protection. The operating system protects the information stored in a multiuser computer system.

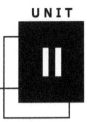

Process Management

Process: A process or task is an instance of a program in execution. The execution of a process must programs in a sequential manner. At any time at most one instruction is executed. The process includes the current activity as represented by the value of the program counter and the content of the processors registers. Also it includes the process stack which contain temporary data (such as method parameters return address and local variables) & a data section which contain global variables.

Difference Between Process & Program

A program by itself is not a process. A program in execution is known as a process. A program is a passive entity, such as the contents of a file stored on disk where as process is an active entity with a program counter specifying the next instruction to execute and a set of associated resources may be shared among several process with some scheduling algorithm being used to determinate when the stop work on one process and service a different one.

Process state: As a process executes, it changes state. The state of a process is defined by the correct activity of that process. Each process may be in one of the following states.

- **New:** The process is being created.
- **Ready:** The process is waiting to be assigned to a processor.
- **Running:** Instructions are being executed.

- **Waiting:** The process is waiting for some event to occur.
- **Terminated:** The process has finished execution.

Many processes may be in ready and waiting state at the same time. But only one process can be running on any processor at any instant.

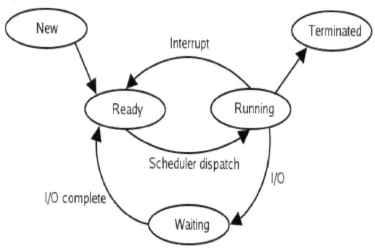

Process Scheduling

Scheduling is a fundamental function of OS. When a computer is multi-programmed, it has multiple processes completing for the CPU at the same time. If only one CPU is available, then a choice has to be made regarding which process to execute next. This decision making process is known as scheduling and the part of the OS that makes this choice is called a scheduler. The algorithm it uses in making this choice is called scheduling algorithm.

Scheduling queues: As processes enter the system, they are put into a job queue. This queue consists of all process in the system. The process that are residing in main memory and are ready & waiting to execute or kept on a list called ready queue.

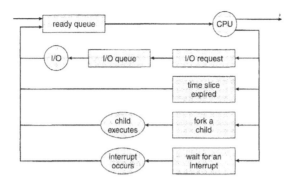

This queue is generally stored as a linked list. A ready queue header contains pointers to the first & final PCB in the list. The PCB includes a pointer field that points to the next PCB in the ready queue. The lists of processes waiting for a particular I/O device are kept on a list called device queue. Each device has its own device queue. A new process is initially put in the ready queue. It waits in the ready queue until it is selected for execution & is given the CPU.

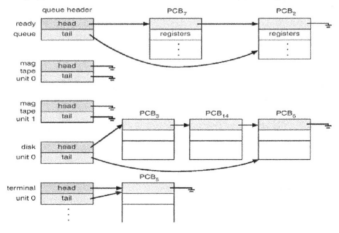

Schedulers

A process migrates between the various scheduling queues throughout its life-time purposes. The OS must select for scheduling processes from these queues in some fashion. This selection process is carried out by the appropriate scheduler. In a batch system, more processes are submitted and then executed immediately. So these processes are spooled to a mass storage device like disk, where they are kept for later execution.

Types of Schedulers

There are 3 types of schedulers mainly used:

1. **Long term scheduler:** Long term scheduler selects process from the disk & loads them into memory for execution. It controls the degree of multi-programming i.e. no. of processes in memory. It executes less frequently than other schedulers. If the degree of multiprogramming is stable than the average rate of process creation is equal to the average departure rate of processes leaving the system. So, the long term scheduler is needed to be invoked only when a process leaves the system. Due to longer intervals between executions it can afford to take more time to decide which process should be selected for execution. Most processes in the CPU are either I/O bound or CPU bound. An I/O bound process (an interactive 'C' program is one that spends most of its time in I/O operation than it spends in doing I/O operation. A CPU bound process is one that spends more of its time in doing computations than I/O operations (complex sorting program). It is important that the long term scheduler should select a good mix of I/O bound & CPU bound processes.

2. **Short term scheduler:** The short term scheduler selects among the process that are ready to execute & allocates the CPU to one of them. The primary distinction between these two schedulers is the frequency of their execution. The short-term scheduler must select a new process for the

CPU quite frequently. It must execute at least one in 100ms. Due to the short duration of time between executions, it must be very fast.

3. **Medium – term scheduler:** some operating systems introduce an additional intermediate level of scheduling known as medium – term scheduler. The main idea behind this scheduler is that sometimes it is advantageous to remove processes from memory & thus reduce the degree of multiprogramming. At some later time, the process can be reintroduced into memory & its execution can be continued from where it had left off. This is called as swapping. The process is swapped out & swapped in later by medium term scheduler. Swapping is necessary to improve theprocess miss or due to some change in memory requirements, the available memory limit is exceeded which requires some memory to be freed up.

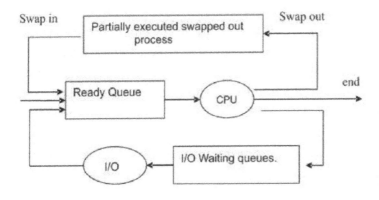

Process Control Block

Each process is represented in the OS by a process control block. It is also by a process control block. It is also known as task control block.

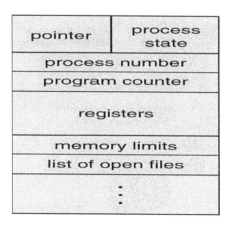

A process control block contains many pieces of information associated with a specific process.

It includes the following information.

- **Process state:** The state may be new, ready, running, waiting or terminated state.
- **Program counter:** it indicates the address of the next instruction to be executed for this purpose.
- **CPU registers:** The registers vary in number & type depending on the computer architecture. It includes accumulators, index registers, stack pointer &general purpose registers, plus any condition – code information must be saved when an interrupt occurs to allow the process to be continued correctly after – ward.
- **CPU scheduling information:** This information includes process priority pointers to scheduling queues & any other scheduling parameters.
- **Memory management information:** This information may include such information as the value of the bar & limit registers, the page tables or the segment tables, depending upon the memory system used by the operating system.
- **Accounting information:** This information includes the amount of CPU and real time used, time limits, account number, job or process numbers and so on.

- **I/O Status Information:** This information includes the list of I/O devices allocated to this process, a list of open files and so on. The PCB simply serves as the repository for any information that may vary from process to process.

CPU Scheduling Algorithm

CPU Scheduling deals with the problem of deciding which of the processes in the ready queue is to be allocated first to the CPU. There are four types of CPU scheduling that exist.

1. **First Come, First Served Scheduling (FCFS) Algorithm:** This is the simplest CPU scheduling algorithm. In this scheme, the process which requests the CPU first, that is allocated to the CPU first. The implementation of the FCFS algorithm is easily managed with a FIFO queue. When a process enters the ready queue its PCB is linked onto the rear of the queue. The average waiting time under FCFS policy is quiet long. Consider the following example:

Process	CPU time
P_1	3
P_2	5
P_3	2
P_4	4

Using FCFS algorithm find the average waiting time and average turnaround time if the order is

P_1, P_2, P_3, P_4.

Solution: If the process arrived in the order P_1, P_2, P_3, P_4 then according to the FCFS the Gantt chart will be:

P_1	P_2	P_3	P_4

0   3   8   10   14

The waiting time for process $P_1 = 0$, $P_2 = 3$, $P_3 = 8$, $P_4 = 10$ then the turnaround time for process $P_1 = 0 + 3 = 3$, $P_2 = 3 + 5 = 8$, $P_3 = 8 + 2 = 10$, $P_4 = 10 + 4 = 14$.

Then average waiting time $= (0 + 3 + 8 + 10)/4 = 21/4 = 5.25$

Average turnaround time $= (3 + 8 + 10 + 14)/4 = 35/4 = 8.75$

The FCFS algorithm is non pre-emptive means once the CPU has been allocated to a process then the process keeps the CPU until the release the CPU either by terminating or requesting I/O.

2. **Shortest Job First Scheduling (SJF) Algorithm:** This algorithm associates with each process if the CPU is available. This scheduling is also known as shortest next CPU burst, because the scheduling is done by examining the length of the next CPU burst of the process rather than its total length. Consider the following example:

Process	CPU time
P_1	3
P_2	5
P_3	2
P_4	4

Solution: According to the SJF the Gantt chart will be

P_3	P_1	P_2	P_4

1   2   5   9   14

The waiting time for process $P_1 = 0$, $P_2 = 2$, $P_3 = 5$, $P_4 = 9$ then the turnaround time for process $P_3 = 0 + 2 = 2$, $P_1 = 2 + 3 = 5$, $P_4 = 5 + 4 = 9$, $P_2 = 9 + 5 = 14$.

Then average waiting time $= (0 + 2 + 5 + 9)/4 = 16/4 = 4$

Average turnaround time = (2 + 5 + 9 + 14)/4 = 30/4 = 7.5

The SJF algorithm may be either preemptive or non preemptive algorithm. The preemptive SJF is also known as shortest remaining time first.

Consider the following example.

Process	Arrival Time	CPU time
P_1	0	8
P_2	1	4
P_3	2	9
P_4	3	5

In this case the Gantt chart will be

P1	P2	P4	P1	P3

0   1   5   10   17   26

The waiting time for process

$P_1 = 10 - 1 = 9$

$P_2 = 1 - 1 = 0$

$P_3 = 17 - 2 = 15$

$P_4 = 5 - 3 = 2$

The average waiting time = (9 + 0 + 15 + 2)/4 = 26/4 = 6.5

3. **Priority Scheduling Algorithm:** In this scheduling a priority is associated with each process and the CPU is allocated to the process with the highest priority. Equal priority processes are scheduled in FCFS manner. Consider the following example:

Process	Arrival Time	CPU time
P_1	10	3
P_2	1	1
P_3	2	3
P_4	1 4	
P_5	5	2

According to the priority scheduling the Gantt chart will be

P2	P5	P1	P3	P4

0   1   6   16   18   19

The waiting time for process

$P_1 = 6$

$P_2 = 0$

$P_3 = 16$

$P_4 = 18$

$P_4 = 1$

The average waiting time $= (0 + 1 + 6 + 16 + 18)/5 = 41/5 = 8.2$

4. **Round Robin Scheduling Algorithm:** This type of algorithm is designed only for the time sharing system. It is similar to FCFS scheduling with preemption condition to switch between processes. A small unit of time called quantum time or time slice is used to switch between the processes. The average waiting time under the round robin policy is quiet long. Consider the following example:

Process	CPU time
P_1	3
P_2	5

P$_3$	2
P$_4$	4

Time Slice = 1 millisecond.

P1	P2	P3	P4		P1	P2	P3	P4	P1	P2	P4	P2	P4	P$_2$
0	1	2	3	4	5	6	7	8	9	10	11	12	13	14

The waiting time for process

$$P_1 = 0 + (4 - 1) + (8 - 5) = 0 + 3 + 3 = 6$$

$$P_2 = 1 + (5 - 2) + (9 - 6) + (11 - 10) + (12 - 11) + (13 - 12) = 1 + 3 + 3 + 1 + 1 + 1 = 10$$

$$P_3 = 2 + (6 - 3) = 2 + 3 = 5$$

$$P_4 = 3 + (7 - 4) + (10 - 8) + (12 - 11) = 3 + 3 + 2 + 1 = 9$$

The average waiting time = (6 + 10 + 5 + 9)/4 = 7.5

Process Synchronization

A co-operation process is one that can affect or be affected by other processes executing in the system. Co-operating process may either directly share a logical address space or be allotted to the shared data only through files. This concurrent access is known as Process synchronization.

Critical Section Problem

Consider a system consisting of n processes (P$_0$, P$_1$, ...P$_{n-1}$) each process has a segment of code which is known as critical section in which the process may be changing common variable, updating a table, writing a file and so on. The important feature of the system is that when the process is executing in its critical section no other process is to be allowed to execute in its critical section. The execution of critical sections by the processes is a mutually exclusive. The critical section problem is to design a protocol that the process can use to cooperate each process must request permission to enter its critical section. The section of code implementing this request is the entry section. The critical section is followed on exit section. The remaining code is the remainder section.

Example:

While (1)
{

    Entry Section;

       Critical Section;

    Exit Section;

       Remainder Section;

}

A solution to the critical section problem must satisfy the following three conditions.

1. **Mutual Exclusion:** If process P_i is executing in its critical section then no any other process can be executing in their critical section.
2. **Progress:** If no process is executing in its critical section and some process wish to enter their critical sections then only those process that are not executing in their remainder section can enter its critical section next.
3. **Bounded waiting:** There exists a bound on the number of times that other processes are allowed to enter their critical sections after a process has made a request.

Semaphores

For the solution to the critical section problem one synchronization tool is used which is known as semaphores. A semaphore 'S' is an integer variable which is accessed through two standard operations such as wait and signal. These operations were originally termed 'P' (for wait means to test) and 'V' (for single means to increment). The classical definition of wait is

```
Wait (S)
{
    While (S <= 0)
{
    Test;
}
    S--;
}
```

The classical definition of the signal is

```
Signal (S)
{
    S++;
}
```

In case of wait the test condition is executed with interruption and the decrement is executed without interruption.

Binary Semaphore

A binary semaphore is a semaphore with an integer value which can range between 0 and 1. Let 'S' be a counting semaphore. To implement the binary semaphore we need following the structure of data. Binary Semaphores S_1, S_2; int C;

Initially S_1 = 1, S2 = 0 and the value of C is set to the initial value of the counting semaphore 'S'.

Then the wait operation of the binary semaphore can be implemented as follows.

Wait (S_1)

C--; if (C < 0)

{

Signal (S_1);

Wait (S_2);

}

Signal (S_1);

The signal operation of the binary semaphore can be implemented as follows:

Wait (S_1);

C++;

if (C <=0)

Signal (S_2);

Else

Signal (S_1);

Classical Problems of Synchronization

There are various types of problem which are proposed for synchronization scheme such as

- **Bounded Buffer Problem:** This problem was commonly used to illustrate the power of synchronization primitives. In this scheme we assumed that the pool consists of 'N' buffer and each capable of holding one item. The 'mutex' semaphore provides mutual exclusion for access to the buffer pool and is initialized to the value one. The empty and full semaphores count the number of empty and full buffer respectively. The semaphore empty is initialized to 'N' and the semaphore full is initialized to zero. This problem is known as procedure and consumer problem. The code of the producer is producing full buffer and the code of consumer is producing empty buffer. The structure of producer process is as follows:

do { produce an item in nextp

. . . .

Wait (empty);

Wait (mutex);

. . . .

addnextp to buffer

. . . .

Signal (mutex);

Signal (full);

} While (1);

The structure of consumer process is as follows:

do {

Wait (full); Wait

(mutex);

. . . .

Remove an item from buffer to nextc

. . . .

Signal (mutex);

Signal (empty);

. . . .

Consume the item in nextc;

. . . .

} While (1);

- **Reader Writer Problem:** In this type of problem there are two types of process are used such as Reader process and Writer process. The reader process is responsible for only reading and the writer process is responsible for writing. This is an important problem of synchronization which has several variations like oThe simplest one is referred as first reader writer problem which requires that no reader will be kept waiting unless a writer has obtained permission to use the shared object. In other words no reader should wait for other reader to finish because a writer is waiting.
- The second reader writer problem requires that once a writer is ready then the writer performs its write operation as soon as possible.

The structure of a reader process is as follows:

Wait (mutex); Read

count++ ; if (read count == 1)

Wait (wrt);

Signal (mutex);

. . . .

Reading is performed

. . . .

Wait (mutex);

Read count -- ; if (read count == 0)

Signal (wrt);

Signal (mutex);

The structure of the writer process is as follows:

Wait (wrt);

Writing is performed;

Signal (wrt);

- **Dining Philosopher Problem:** Consider 5 philosophers to spend their lives in thinking & eating. A philosopher shares common circular table surrounded by 5 chairs each occupies by one philosopher. In the center of the table there is a bowl of rice and the table is laid with 6 chopsticks as shown in below figure.

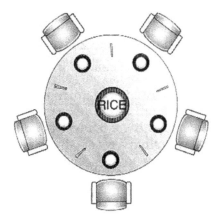

When a philosopher thinks she does not interact with her colleagues. From time to time a philosopher gets hungry and tries to pickup two chopsticks that are closest to her. A philosopher may pickup one chopstick or two chopsticks at a time but she cannot pickup a chopstick that is already in hand of the neighbor. When a hungry philosopher has both her chopsticks at the same time, she eats without releasing her chopsticks. When she finished eating, she puts down both of her chopsticks and starts thinking again. This problem is considered as classic synchronization problem. According to this problem each chopstick is represented by a semaphore. A philosopher grabs the chopsticks by executing the wait operation on that semaphore. She releases the chopsticks by executing the signal operation on the appropriate semaphore. The structure of dining philosopher is as follows:

```
do{

Wait (chopstick [(i+1)%5]);

. . . . . . . . . . . .

Eat

. . . . . . . . . . . .

Signal (chopstick [i]); Signal (chopstick [(i+1)%5]);

. . . . . . . . . . . .

Think

. . . . . . . . . . . .

} While (1);
```

Critical Region:

According to the critical section problem using semaphore all processes must share a semaphore variablemutex which is initialized to one. Each process must execute wait (mutex) before entering the critical section and execute the signal (mutex) after completing the execution but there are various difficulties may arise with this approach like:

Case 1: Suppose that a process interchanges the order in which the wait and signal operations on the semaphore mutex are executed, resulting in the following execution:

Signal (mutex);

. . . .

Critical Section

. . . .

Wait (mutex);

In this situation several processes may be executing in their critical sections simultaneously, which is violating mutual exclusion requirement.

Case 2: Suppose that a process replaces the signal (mutex) with wait (mutex). The execution is as follows: Wait (mutex);

. . . .

Critical Section

. . . .

Wait (mutex);

In this situation a deadlock will occur

Case 3: Suppose that a process omits the wait (mutex) and the signal (mutex). In this case the mutual exclusion is violated or a deadlock will occur.

To illustrate the various types or error generated by using semaphore there are some high level language constructs have been introduced such as critical region and monitor.

Critical region is also known as conditional critical regions. It constructs guards against certain simple errors associated with semaphore. This high level language synchronization construct requires a variable V of type T which is to be shared among many processes. It is declared as V: shared T;

The variable V can be accessed only inside a region statement as like below:

Wait (mutex);

While (! B) {

First_count++; if

(second_count> 0)

Signal (second_delay);

Else

Signal (mutex);

Wait (first_delay);

First_count--;

Second_count++;

if (first_count> 0)

Signal (first_delay);

Else

Signal (second_delay);

Wait (second_delay);

Second_count – -;

} S;

if (first_count> 0)

Signal (first_delay);

Else if (second_count> 0)

Signal (second_delay);

Else

Signal (mutex);

(Implementation of the Conditional Region Constructs)

Where B is a Boolean variable which governs the access to the critical regions which is initialized to false.Mutex, First_delay and Second_delay are the semaphores which are initialized to 1, 0, and 0 respectively. First_count and Second_count are the integer variables which are initialized to zero.

Monitor

It is characterized as a set of programmer defined operators. Its representation consists of declaring of variables, whose value defines the state of an instance. The syntax of monitor is as follows. Monitor monitor_name

{

Shared variable declarations Procedure body

```
P1 (.........) {

........

}
          Procedure body P2 (.........) { ........

}

.

.

.

Procedure body Pn (.........) {

........

}

{

Initialization Code

}

}
```

Atomic Transaction

This section is related to the field of database system. Atomic transaction describes the various techniques of database and how they are can be used by the operating system. It ensures that the critical sections are executed automatically. To determine how the system should ensure atomicity we need first to identify the properties of the devices used to for storing the data accessed by the transactions. The various types storing devices are as follows:

- **Volatile Storage:** Information residing in volatile storage does not survive in case of system crash. Example of volatile storage is main memory and cache memory.

- **Non volatile Storage:** Information residing in this type of storage usually survives in case of system crash. Examples are Magnetic Disk, Magnetic Tape and Hard Disk.
- **Stable Storage:** Information residing in stable storage is never lost. Example is non volatile cache memory.

The various techniques used for ensuring the atomicity are as follows:

1. **Log based Recovery:** This technique is used for achieving the atomicity by using data structure called log. A log has the following fields:

   a. **Transaction Name:** This is the unique name of the transaction that performed the write operation.
   b. **Data Item Name:** This is the unique name given to the data.
   c. **Old Value:**This is the value of the data before to the write operation.
   d. **New value:** This is the value of the data after the write operation.

This recovery technique uses two processes such as Undo and Redo. Undo restores the value of old data updated by a transaction to the old values. Redo sets the value of the data updated by a transaction to the new values.

2. **Checkpoint:** In this principle system maintains the log. The checkpoint requires the following sequences of action.

   a. Output all the log records from volatile storage into stable storage.
   b. Output all modified data residing in volatile to the stable storage.
   c. Output a checkpoint onto the stable storage.

T_0	T_1
Read (A)	
Write (A)	
Read (B)	

Write (B)

transaction Read (A) system Write (A) read and Read (B) their Write (B)

3. **Serializibility:** In this technique the executed serially in some arbitrary order. Consider a consisting two data items A and B which are both written by two transactions T0 and T1. Suppose that transactions are executed automatically in the order

T_0 followed by T_1. This execution sequence is known as schedule which is represented as below.

If transactions are overlapped then their execution resulting schedule is known as non-serial scheduling or concurrent schedule as like below:

T_0	T_1
Read (A)	
Write (A)	
	Read (A)
	Write (A)
Read (B)	
Write (B)	
	Read (B)
	Write (B)

4. **Locking:** This technique governs how the locks are acquired and released. There are two types of lock such as shared lock and exclusive lock. If a transaction T has obtained a shared lock (S) on data item Q then T can read this item but cannot write. If a transaction T has obtained an exclusive lock (S) on data item Q then T can both read and write in the data item Q.

5. **Timestamp:** In this technique each transaction in the system is associated with unique fixed timestamp denoted by TS. This timestamp is assigned by the system before the transaction starts. If a transaction T_i has been assigned with a timestamp TS (T_i) and later a new transaction T_j enters the system then TS (T_i) <TS (T_j). There are two types of timestamp such as Wtimestamp and R-timestamp. W-timestamp denotes the largest timestamp of any transaction that performed write operation successfully. R-timestamp denotes the largest timestamp of any transaction that executed read operation successfully.

Deadlock

In a multiprogramming environment several processes may compete for a finite number of resources. A process request resources; if the resource is available at that time a process enters the wait state. Waiting process may never change its state because the resources requested are held by other waiting process. This situation is known as deadlock.

Example

- System has 2 disk drives.
- P1 and P2 each hold one disk drive and each needs another one.
- 2 train approaches each other at crossing, both will come to full stop and neither shall start until other has gone.

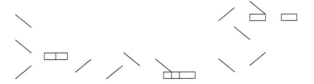

- Traffic only in one direction.
- Each section of a bridge can be viewed as a resource.
- If a deadlock occurs, it can be resolved if one car backs up (preempt resources and rollback).
- Several cars may have to be backed up if a deadlock occurs.
- Starvation is possible

System Model

A system consists of a finite number of resources to be distributed among a number of competing processes. The resources are partitioned into several types each of which consists of a number of identical instances. A process may utilized a resources in the following sequence

- **Request:** In this state one can request a resource.
- **Use:** In this state the process operates on the resource.
- **Release:** In this state the process releases the resources.

Deadlock Characteristics: In a deadlock process never finish executing and system resources are tied up. A deadlock situation can arise if the following four conditions hold simultaneously in a system.

- **Mutual Exclusion:** At a time only one process can use the resources. If another process requests that resource, requesting process must wait until the resource has been released.
- **Hold and wait:** A process must be holding at least one resource and waiting to additional resource that is currently held by other processes.
- **No Preemption:** Resources allocated to a process can't be forcibly taken out from it unless it releases that resource after completing the task.
- **Circular Wait:** A set $\{P_0, P_1, \ldots\ldots P_n\}$ of waiting state/ process must exists such that P_0 is waiting for a resource that is held by P_1, P_1 is waiting for the resource that is held by $P_2 \ldots\ldots P_{(n-1)}$ is waiting for the resource that is held by P_n and P_n is waiting for the resources that is held by P_4.

Resource Allocation Graph

Deadlock can be described more clearly by directed graph which is called system resource allocation graph. The graph consists of a set of vertices 'V' and a set of edges 'E'. The set of vertices 'V' is partitioned into two different types of nodes such as P = {P_1, P_2, ...P_n}, the set of all the active processes in the system and R = {R_1, R_2, ...R_m}, the set of all the resource type in the system. A directed edge from process P_i to resource type R_j is denoted by P_i → R_j. It signifies that process P_i is an instance of resource type R_j and waits for that resource. A directed edge from resource type R_j to the process P_i which signifies that an instance of resource type R_j has been allocated to process P_i. A directed edge P_i → R_j is called as request edge and R_j → P_i is called as assigned edge.

- Process

- Resource Type with 4 instances

- P_i requests instance of R_j

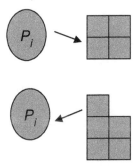

- P_i is holding an instance of R_j

When a process P_i requests an instance of resource type R_j then a request edge is inserted as resource allocation graph. When this request can be fulfilled, the request edge is transformed to an assignment edge. When the process no longer needs access to the resource it releases the resource and as a result the assignment edge is deleted. The resource allocation graph shown in below figure has the following situation.

- The sets P, R, E

$P = \{P_1, P_2, P_3\}$

$R = \{R_1, R_2, R_3, R_4\}$

$E = \{P_1 \rightarrow R_1, P_2 \rightarrow R_3, R_1 \rightarrow P_2, R_2 \rightarrow P_2, R_2 \rightarrow P_1, R_3 \rightarrow P_3\}$

The resource instances are Resource R_1 has one instance

Resource R_2 has two instances.
Resource R_3 has one instance
Resource R_4 has three instances.

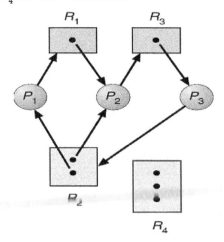

The process states are:

Process P_1 is holding an instance of R_2 and waiting for an instance of R_1.

Process P_2 is holding an instance of R_1 and R_2 and waiting for an instance R_3.

Process P_3 is holding an instance of R_3.

The following example shows the resource allocation graph with a deadlock.

P1 – > R1 – > P2 – > R3 – > P3 – > R2 – > P1
P2 – > R3 – > P3 – > R2 – >P1

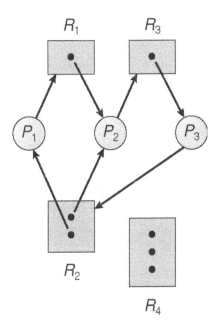

The following example shows the resource allocation graph with a cycle but no deadlock.

P1 – > R1 – > P3 – > R2 – > P1

No deadlock

P4 may release its instance of resource R2

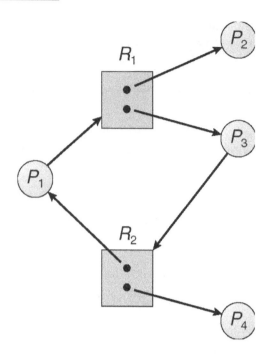

The problem of deadlock can deal with the following 3 ways.

We can use a protocol to prevent or avoid deadlock ensuring that the system will never enter to a deadlock state.

We can allow the system to enter a deadlock state, detect it and recover.

We can ignore the problem all together.

To ensure that deadlock never occur the system can use either a deadlock prevention or deadlock avoidance scheme.

Deadlock Prevention

Deadlock prevention is a set of methods for ensuring that at least one of these necessary conditions cannot hold.

Mutual Exclusion: The mutual exclusion condition holds for non sharable. The example is a printer cannot be simultaneously shared by several processes. Sharable resources do not require mutual exclusive access and thus cannot be involved in a dead lock. The example is read only files which are in sharing condition. If several processes attempt to open the read only file at the same time they can be guaranteed simultaneous access.

Hold and wait: To ensure that the hold and wait condition never occurs in the system, we must guaranty that whenever a process requests a resource it does not hold any other resources. There are two protocols to handle these problems such as one protocol that can be used requires each process to request and be allocated all its resources before it begins execution. The other protocol allows a process to request resources only when the process has no resource. These protocols have two main disadvantages. First, resource utilization may be low, since many of the resources may be allocated but unused for a long period. Second, starvation is possible. A process that needs several popular resources may have to wait indefinitely, because at least one of the resources that it needs is always allocated to some other process.

No Preemption: To ensure that this condition does not hold, a protocol is used. If a process is holding some resources and request another resource that cannot be immediately allocated to it. The preempted one added to a list of resources for which the process is waiting. The process will restart only when it can regain its old resources, as well as the new ones that it is requesting. Alternatively if a process requests some resources, we first check whether they are available. If they are, we allocate them. If they are not available, we check whether they are allocated to some other process that is waiting for additional resources. If so, we preempt the desired resources from the waiting process and allocate them to the requesting process. If the resources are not either available or held by a waiting process, the requesting process must wait.

Circular Wait: We can ensure that this condition never holds by ordering of all resource type and to require that each process requests resource in an increasing order of enumeration. Let $R = \{R_1, R_2, \ldots\ldots R_n\}$ be the set of resource types. We assign to each resource type a unique integer number, which allows us to compare two resources and to determine whether one precedes another in our ordering. Formally, we define a one to one function $F: R \to N$, where N is the set of natural numbers. For example, if the set of resource types R includes tape drives, disk drives and printers, then the function F might be defined as follows:

F (Tape Drive) = 1,

F (Disk Drive) = 5,

F (Printer) = 12.

We can now consider the following protocol to prevent deadlocks: Each process can request resources only in an increasing order of enumeration. That is, a process can initially request any number of instances of a resource type, say R_i. After that, the process can request instances of resource type R_j if and only if $F(R_j) > F(R_i)$. If several instances of the same resource type are needed, defined previously, a process that wants to use the tape drive and printer at the same time must first request the tape drive and then request the printer.

Deadlock Avoidance

Requires additional information about how resources are to be used. Simplest and most useful model requires that each process declare the maximum number of resources of each type that it may need. The deadlock-avoidance algorithm dynamically examines the resource-allocation state to ensure that there can never be a circular-wait condition. Resource-allocation state is defined by the number of available and allocated resources, and the maximum demands of the processes.

Safe State

When a process requests an available resource, system must decide if immediate allocation leaves the system in a safe state. Systems are in safe state if there exists a safe sequence of all process. A sequence $<P_1, P_2, ..., P_n>$ of ALL the processes is the system such that for each P_i, the resources that P_i can still request can be satisfied by currently available resources + resources held by all the P_j, with $j < i$. That is:

- If P_i resource needs are not immediately available, then P_i can wait until all P_j have finished.
- When P_j is finished, P_i can obtain needed resources, execute, return allocated resources, and terminate.
- When P_i terminates, P_{i+1} can obtain its needed resources, and so on.
- If system is in safe state => No deadlock
- If system in not in safe state => possibility of deadlock
- OS cannot prevent processes from requesting resources in a sequence that leads to deadlock
- Avoidance => ensue that system will never enter an unsafe state, prevent getting into deadlock

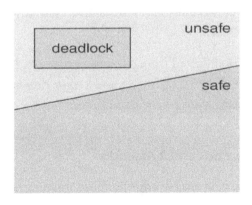

	Maximum Needs	Current Needs
P_0	10	5
P_1	4	2
P_2	9	2

- Suppose processes P0, P1, and P2 share 12 magnetic tape drives
- Currently 9 drives are held among the processes and 3 are available
- Question: Is this system currently in a safe state?
- Answer: Yes!

Safe Sequence: <P1, P0, P2>

	Maximum Needs	Current Needs
P_0	10	5
P_1	4	2
P_2	9	2

- Suppose process P2 requests and is allocated 1 more tape drive.
- Question: Is the resulting state still safe?
- Answer: No! Because there does not exist a safe sequence anymore.

Only P1 can be allocated its maximum needs.
IFP0 and P2 request 5 more drives and 6 more drives, respectively, then the resulting state will be deadlocked.

Resource Allocation Graph Algorithm

In this graph a new type of edge has been introduced is known as claim edge. Claim edge $P_i \rightarrow R_j$ indicates that process P_j may request resource R_j; represented by a dashed line. Claim edge converts to request edge when a process requests a resource.Request edge converted to an assignment edge when the resource is allocated to the process.When a resource is released by a process, assignment edge reconverts to a claim edge.Resources must be claimed a priori in the system.

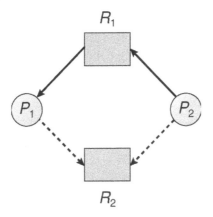

P2 requesting R1, but R1 is already allocated to P1.
  Both processes have a claim on resource R2
  What happens if P2 now requests resource R2?

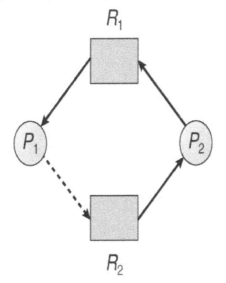

Cannot allocate resource R2 to process P2
   Why? Because resulting state is unsafe

- P1 could request R2, thereby creating deadlock!

Use only when there is a single instance of each resource type
- Suppose that process P_i requests a resource R_j
- The request can be granted only if converting the request edge to an assignment edge does not result in the formation of a cycle in the resource allocation graph.
- Here we check for safety by using cycle-detection algorithm.

Banker's Algorithm

This algorithm can be used in banking system to ensure that the bank never allocates all its available cash such that it can no longer satisfy the needs of all its customer. This algorithm is applicable to a system with multiple instances of each resource type. When a new process enter in to the system it must declare the maximum number of instances of each resource type that it may need. This number may not exceed the total number of resources in the system. Several data structure must be maintained to implement the banker's algorithm. Let,

- n = number of processes
- m = number of resources types

Available: Vector of length m. If Available[j] = k, there are k instances of resource type R_j available.

Max: n x m matrix. If Max [i,j] = k, then process P_i may request at most k instances of resource type R_j.

Allocation: n x m matrix. If Allocation[i,j] = k then P_i is currently allocated k instances of R_j.

Need: n x m matrix. If Need[i,j] = k, then P_i may need k more instances of R_j to complete its task.

Need [i,j] = Max[i,j] – Allocation [i,j].

Safety Algorithm

1. Let Workand Finish be vectors of length m and n, respectively. Initialize: Work = Available

   Finish [i] = false for i = 0, 1, ...,n – 1.

2. Find and i such that both:

   a. Finish [i] = false
   b. $Need_i \leq Work$

If no such i exists, go to step 4.

3. Work = Work + $Allocation_i$ Finish[i] = true go to step 2.

4. If Finish [i] == true for all i, then the system is in a safe state.

Resource Allocation Algorithm

Request = request vector for process P_i. If $Request_i[j]$ = k then process P_i wants k instances of resource type R_j.

1. If $Request_i \leq Need_i$ go to step 2. Otherwise, raise error condition, since process has exceeded its maximum claim.
2. If $Request_i \leq Available$, go to step 3. Otherwise P_i must wait, since resources are not available.
3. Pretend to allocate requested resources to P_i by modifying the state as follows:

Available = Available – Request;

   $Allocation_i$ = $Allocation_i$ + $Request_i$;

   $Need_i = Need_i$ – $Request_i$;

- If safe ⇒ the resources are allocated to Pi.
- If unsafe ⇒ Pi must wait, and the old resource-allocation state is restored

Example

- 5 processes P_0 through P_4;
- 3 resource types:

  A (10 instances), B (5instances), and C (7 instances).

- Snapshot at time T_0:

	Allocation A B C	Max A B C	Available A B C
P0	0 1 0	7 5 3	3 3 2
P1	2 0 0	3 2 2	
P_2	3 0 2	9 0 2	
P_3	2 1 1	2 2 2	
P_4	0 0 2	4 3 3	

- The content of the matrix Need is defined to be Max – Allocation.

	Need A B C
P0	7 4 3
P1	1 2 2
P_2	6 0 0
P_3	0 1 1
P_4	4 3 1

- The system is in a safe state since the sequence $<P_1, P_3, P_4, P_2, P_0>$ satisfies safety criteria.

  P_1 requests $(1, 0, 2)$

- Check that Request ≤ Available (that is, $(1,0,2) \leq (3,3,2) \Rightarrow$ true.

Allocation		Need	Available
		A B C	A B C A B C
	P_0	0 1 0	7 4 3 2 3 0
	P_1	3 0 2	0 2 0
	P_2	3 0 1	6 0 0
	P_3	2 1 1	0 1 1
	P_4	0 0 2	4 3 1

- Executing safety algorithm shows that sequence $<P_1, P_3, P_4, P_0, P_2>$ satisfies safety requirement.
- Can request for $(3,3,0)$ by P_4 be granted? –NO
- Can request for $(0,2,0)$ by P_0 be granted? –NO (Results Unsafe)

Deadlock Detection

If a system doesn't employ either a deadlock prevention or deadlock avoidance, then deadlock situation may occur. In this environment the system must provide

- An algorithm to recover from the deadlock.
- An algorithm to remove the deadlock is applied either to a system which pertains single in instance each resource type or a system which pertains several instances of a resource type.

Single Instance of Each Resource Type

If all resources only a single instance then we can define a deadlock detection algorithm which uses a new form of resource allocation graph called "Wait for graph". We obtain this graph from the resource allocation graph by removing the nodes of type resource and collapsing the appropriate edges. The below figure describes the resource allocation graph and corresponding wait for graph.

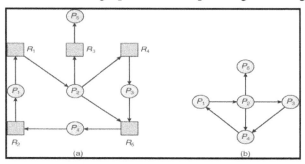

Resource-Allocation   Correspondin
    Graph wait-for graph

- For single instance
- $P_i - >P_j$ (P_i is waiting for P_j to release a resource that P_i needs)
- $P_i ->P_j$ exist if and only if RAG contains 2 edges $P_i - >R_q$ and $R_q - >P_j$ for some resource R_q.

Several Instances of a Resource type

The wait for graph scheme is not applicable to a resource allocation system with multiple instances of reach resource type. For this case the algorithm employs several data structures which are similar to those used in the banker's algorithm like available, allocation and request.

- **Available:** A vector of length m indicates the number of available resources of each type.

- **Allocation**: An n x m matrix defines the number of resources of each type currently allocated to each process.
- **Request**: An n x m matrix indicates the current request of each process. If Request $[i_j]$ = k, then process P_i is requesting k more instances of resource type. R_j.

1. Let Work and Finish be vectors of length m and n, respectively Initialize:

    a. Work = Available
    b. For i = 1,2, ..., n, if Allocation$_i \neq$ 0, then Finish[i] = false;otherwise, Finish[i] = true.

2. Find an index i such that both:

    a. Finish[i] == false
    b. Request$_i \leq$Work

If no such i exists, go to step 4.

3. Work = Work + Allocation
    Finish [i] = true
    Go to step 2

4. If Finish [i] = false, for some i, $1 \leq i \leq$ n, then the system is in a deadlock state. Moreover, if Finish [i] = false, then process P_i is deadlocked.

Recovery from Deadlock

When a detection algorithm determines that a deadlock exists, several alternatives exist. One possibility is to inform the operator that a deadlock has occurred, and to let the operator deal with the deadlock manually. The other possibility is to let the system recover from the deadlock automatically. There are two options for breaking a deadlock. One solution is simply to abort one or more processes to break the circular wait. The second option is to preempt some resources from one or more of the deadlocked processes.

Process Termination

To eliminate deadlocks by aborting a process, we use one of two methods. In both methods, the system reclaims all resources allocated to the terminated processes.

- **Abort all deadlocked processes:** This method clearly will break the deadlock cycle, but at a great expense; these processes may have computed for a long time, and the results of these partial computations must be discarded and probably recomputed later.
- **Abort one process at a time until the deadlock cycle is eliminated:**This method incurs considerable overhead, since after each process is aborted, a deadlock detection algorithm must be invoked to determine whether any processes are still deadlocked.

Resource Preemption

To eliminate deadlocks using resource preemption, we successively preempt some resources from processes and give these resources to other processes until the deadlock cycle is broken. If preemption is required to deal with deadlocks, then three issues need to be addressed.

- **Selecting a victim:** Which resources and which processes are to be preempted? As in process termination, we must determine the order of preemption to minimize cost. Cost factors may include such parameters as the numbers of resources a deadlock process is holding, and the amount of time a deadlocked process has thus far consumed during its execution.

- **Rollback:** If we preempt a resource from a process, what should be done with that process? Clearly, it cannot continue with its normal execution; it is missing some needed resource. We must rollback the process to some safe state, and restart it from that state.

- **Starvation:** In a system where victim selection is based primarily on cost factors, it may happen that the same process is always picked as a victim. As a result, this process never completes its designated task, a starvation situation that needs to be dealt with in any practical system. Clearly, we must ensure that a process can be picked as a victim only a small finite number of times. The most common solution is to include the number of rollbacks in the cost factor.

Memory Management

- Memory consists of a large array of words or bytes, each with its own address. The CPU fetches instructions from memory according to the value of the program counter. These instructions may cause additional loading from and storing to specific memory addresses.
- Memory unit sees only a stream of memory addresses. It does not know how they are generated.
- Program must be brought into memory and placed within a process for it to be run.
- Input queue – collection of processes on the disk that are waiting to be brought into memory for execution.
- User programs go through several steps before being run.

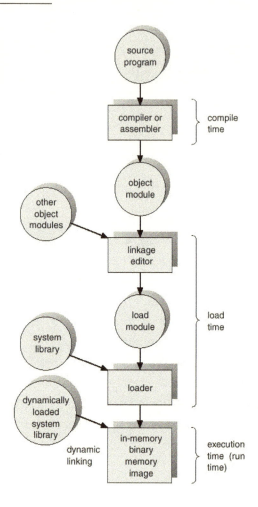

Address binding of instructions and data to memory addresses can happen at three different stages.

- **Compile time**: If memory location known a priori, absolute code can be generated; must recompile code if starting location changes.

Example: .COM-format programs in MS-DOS.

- **Load time**: Must generate relocatable code if memory location is not known at compile time.

- **Execution time**: Binding delayed until run time if the process can be moved during its execution from one memory segment to another. Need hardware support for address maps (e.g., relocation registers).

Logical Versus Physical Address Space

- The concept of a logical address space that is bound to a separate physicaladdress space is central to proper memory management.

  - Logical address – address generated by the CPU; also referred to as virtual address. oPhysical address – address seen by the memory unit.

- The set of all logical addresses generated by a program is a logical address space; the set of all physical addresses corresponding to these logical addresses are a physical address space.
- Logical and physical addresses are the same in compile-time and load-time address-binding schemes; logical (virtual) and physical addresses differ in execution-time address-binding scheme.
- The run-time mapping from virtual to physical addresses is done by a hardware device called the the memory management unit (MMU).

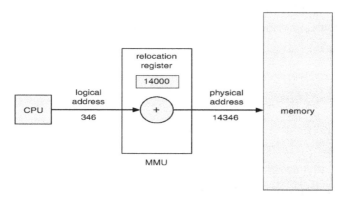

- This method requires hardware support slightly different from the hardware configuration. The base register is now called a relocation register. The value in the relocation register is added to every address generated by a user process at the time it is sent to memory.
- The user program never sees the real physical addresses. The program can create a pointer to location 346, store it in memory, manipulate it and compare it to other addresses. The user program deals with logical addresses. The memory mapping hardware converts logical addresses into physical addresses. The final location of a referenced memory address is not determined until the reference is made.

Dynamic Loading

- Routine is not loaded until it is called.
- All routines are kept on disk in arelocatable load format.
- The main program is loaded into memory and is executed. When a routine needs to call another routine, the calling routine first checks to see whether the other the desired routine into memory and to update the program's address tables to reflect this change. Then control is passed to the newly loaded routine.
- Better memory-space utilization; unused routine is never loaded.
- Useful when large amounts of code are needed to handle infrequently occurring cases.
- No special support from the operating system is required.
- Implemented through program design.

Dynamic Linking

- Linking is postponed until execution time.
- Small piece of code, stub, is used to locate the appropriate memory-resident library routine, or to load the library if the routine is not already present.

- When this stub is executed, it checks to see whether the needed routine is already in memory. If not, the program loads the routine into memory.
- Stub replaces itself with the address of the routine, and executes the routine.
- Thus the next time that code segment is reached, the library routine is executed directly, incurring no cost for dynamic linking.
- Operating system is needed to check if routine is in processes' memory address.
- Dynamic linking is particularly useful for libraries.

Swapping

- A process can be swapped temporarily out of memory to a backing store, and then brought back into memory for continued execution. For example, assume a multiprogramming environment with a round robin CPU scheduling algorithm. When a quantum expires, the memory manager will start to swap out the process that just finished, and to swap in another process to the memory space that has been freed. In the mean time, the CPU scheduler will allocate a time slice to some other process in memory. When each process finished its quantum, it will be swapped with another process. Ideally, the memory manager can swap processes fast enough that some processes will be in memory, ready to execute, when the CPU scheduler wants to reschedule the CPU. The quantum must also be sufficiently large that reasonable amounts of computing are done between swaps.
- Roll out, roll in – swapping variant used for priority-based scheduling algorithms. If a higher priority process arrives and wants service, the memory manager can swap out the lower

priority process so that it can load and execute lower priority process can be swapped back in and continued. This variant is some times called roll out, roll in. Normally a process that is swapped out will be swapped back into the same memory space that it occupied previously. This restriction is dictated by the process cannot be moved to different locations. If execution time binding is being used, then a process can be swapped into a different memory space, because the physical addresses are computed during execution time.

- Backing store – fast disk large enough to accommodate copies of all memory images for all users; must provide direct access to these memory images. It must be large enough to accommodate copies of all memory images for all users, and it must provide direct access to these memory images. The system maintains a ready queue consisting of all processes whose memory images are scheduler decides to execute a process it calls the dispatcher. The dispatcher checks to see whether the next process in the queue is in memory. If not, and there is no free memory region, the dispatcher swaps out a process currently in memory and swaps in the desired process. It then reloads registers as normal and transfers control to the selected process.

- Major part of swap time is transfer time; total transfer time is directly proportional to the amount of memory swapped.

- Modified versions of swapping are found on many systems (i.e., UNIX, Linux, and Windows).

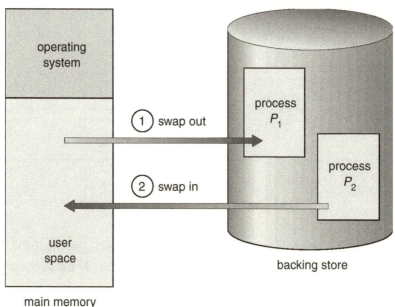

main memory

Contiguous Memory Allocation

- Main memory is usually divided into two partitions:

  - Resident operating system, usually held in low memory with interrupt vector. oUser processes, held in high memory.

- In contiguous memory allocation, each process is contained in a single contiguous section of memory.
- Single-partition allocation oRelocation-register scheme used to protect user processes from each other, and from changing operating-system code and data.

  - Relocation register contains value of smallest physical address; limit register contains range of logical addresses – each logical address must be less than the limit register.

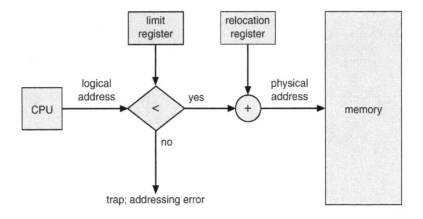

- Multiple-partition allocation oHole – block of available memory; holes of various size are scattered throughout memory.

  - When a process arrives, it is allocated memory from a hole large enough to accommodate it. oOperating system maintains information about:

    a) allocated partitions b) free partitions (hole)

  - A set of holes of various sizes, is scattered throughout memory at any given time. When a process arrives and needs memory, the system searches this set for a hole that is large enough for this process. If the hole is too large, it is split into two: one part is allocated to the arriving process; the other is returned to the set of holes. When a process terminates, it releases its block of memory, which is then placed back in the set of holes. If the new hold is adjacent to other holes, these adjacent holes are merged to form one larger hole.

  - This procedure is a particular instance of the general dynamic storage allocation problem, which is how to satisfy a request of size n from a list of free holes. There are many solutions to this problem. The set of holes is searched to determine which hole is best to allocate. The first-fit, best-fit and worst-fit strategies are the most common ones used to select a free hole from the set of available holes.

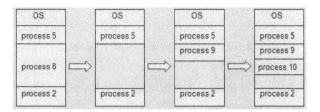

- **First-fit:** Allocate the first hole that is big enough.
- **Best-fit:** Allocate the smallest hole that is big enough; must search entire list, unless ordered by size.
- **Worst-fit:** Allocate the largest hole; must also search entire list.

Fragmentation

- **External Fragmentation** – total memory space exists to satisfy a request, but it is not contiguous.
- **Internal Fragmentation** – allocated memory may be slightly larger than requested memory; this size difference is memory internal to a partition, but not being used.
- Reduce external fragmentation by compaction oShuffle memory contents to place all free memory together in one large block.
  - Compaction is possible only if relocation is dynamic, and is done at execution time.

Paging

- Paging is a memory management scheme that permits the physical address space of a process to be non contiguous.

- Divide physical memory into fixed-sized blocks called **frames** (size is power of 2, for example 512 bytes).
- Divide logical memory into blocks of same size called **pages**. When a process is to be executed, its pages are loaded into any available memory frames from the backing store. The backing store is divided into fixed sized blocks that are of the same size as the memory frames.
- The hardware support for paging is illustrated in below figure.
- Every address generated by the CPU is divided into two parts: a page number (p) and a page offset (d). The page number is used as an index into a page table. The page table contains the base address of each page in physical memory. This base address is combined with the page offset to define the physical memory address that is sent to the memory unit.

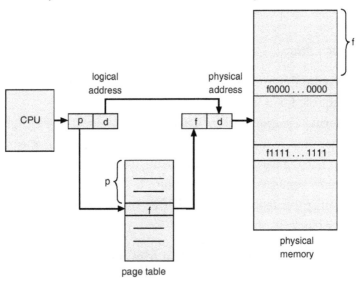

- The paging model of memory is shown in below figure. The page size is defined by the hardware. The size of a page is typically of a power of 2, varying between 512 bytes and 16 MB per page, depending on the computer architecture. The selection of a power of 2 as a page size makes the translation of a logical address into a page number and page offset particularly easy. If the size of logical address is 2^m, and a page size is 2^n addressing units, then the high order m-n bits of a logical address designate the page number, and the n low order bits designate the page

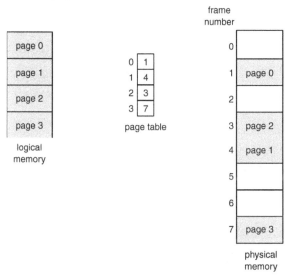

- To run a program of size n pages, need to find n free frames and load program.
- Set up a page table to translate logical to physical addresses.
- Internal fragmentation may occur.

Let us take an example. Suppose a program needs 32 KB memory for allocation. The whole program is divided into smaller units assuming 4 KB and is assigned some address. The address consists of two parts such as:

- A large number in higher order positions and
- Displacement or offset in the lower order bits.

The numbers allocated to pages are typically in power of 2 to simplify extraction of page numbers and offsets. To access a piece of data at a given address, the system first extracts the page number and the offset. Then it translates the page number to physical page frame and access data at offset in physical page frame. At this moment, the translation of the address by the OS is done using a page table. Page table is a linear array indexed by virtual page number which provides the physical page frame that contains the particular page. It employs a lookup process that extracts the page number and the offset. The system in addition checks that the page number is within the address space of process and retrieves the page number in the page table. Physical address will calculated by using the formula.

Physical address = page size of logical memory X frame number + offset

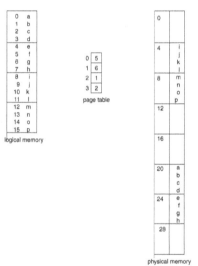

physical memory

When a process arrives in the system to be executed, its size expressed in pages is examined. Each page of the process needs one frame. Thus if the process requires n pages, at least n frames must be available in memory. If n frames are available, they are allocated to this arriving process. The first page of the process is loaded into one of the allocated frames, and the frame number is put in the page table for this process. The next page is loaded into another frame, and its frame number is put into the page table and so on as in below figure. An important aspect of paging is the clear separation between the user's view of memory and the actual physical memory. The user program views that memory as one single contiguous space, containing only this one program. In fact, the user program is scattered throughout physical memory, which also holds other programs. The difference between the user's view of memory and the actual physical memory is reconciled by the address-translation hardware. The logical addresses are translated into physical addresses. This mapping is hidden from the user and is controlled by the operating system.

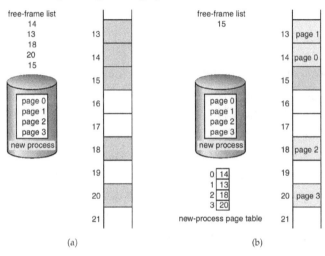

(a)   (b)

- Page table is kept in main memory.
- Page-tablebase register (PTBR) points to the page table.
- In this scheme every data/instruction-byte access requires two memory accesses. One for the page-table entry and one for the byte.
- The two memory access problem can be solved by the use of a special fast-lookup hardware cache called associative registers or associative memory or translation look-aside buffers(TLBs).
- Typically, the number of entries in a TLB is between 32 and 1024.

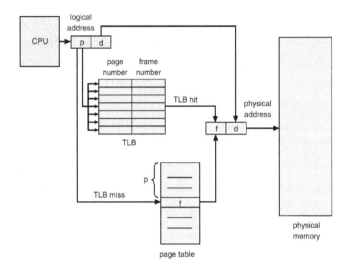

page table

- The TLB contains only a few of the page table entries. When a logical address is generated by the CPU, its page number is presented to the TLB. If the page number is found, its frame number is immediately available and is used to access memory. The whole task may take less than 10 percent longer than it would if an unmapped memory reference were used.
- If the page number is not in the TLB (known as a TLB miss), a memory reference to the page table must be made. When the frame number is obtained, we can use it to access memory.

Hit Ratio

- Hit Ratio: the percentage of times that a page number is found in the associative registers.
- For example, if it takes 20 nanoseconds to search the associative memory and 100 nanoseconds to access memory; for a 98-percent hit ratio, we have
  Effective memory-access time = 0.98 x 120 + 0.02 x 220 = 122 nanoseconds.
- The Intel 80486 CPU has 32 associative registers, and claims a 98-percent hit ratio.

Valid or invalid bit in a page table

- Memory protection implemented by associating protection bit with each frame.
- Valid-invalid bit attached to each entry in the page table:

  - "Valid" indicates that the associated page is in the process' logical address space, and is thus a legal page.

  - "Invalid" indicates that the page is not in the process' logical address space.

- Pay attention to the following figure. The program extends to only address 10,468, any reference beyond that address is illegal. However, references to page 5 are classified as valid, so accesses to addresses up to 12,287 are valid. This reflects the internal fragmentation of paging.

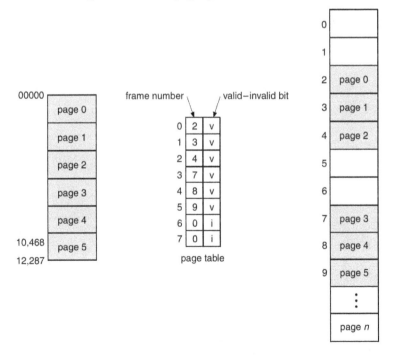

Structure of the Page Table

Hierarchical Paging

- A logical address (on 32-bit machine with 4K page size) is divided into:
  - A page number consisting of 20 bits. oA page offset consisting of 12 bits.

- Since the page table is paged, the page number is further divided into:
  - A 10-bit page number. oA 10-bit page offset.

- Thus, a logical address is as follows:

page number		page offset
p_1	p_2	d
10	10	12

Where p_1 is an index into the outer page table, and p_2 is the displacement within the page of the outer page table. The below figure shows a two level page table scheme.

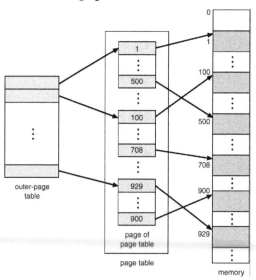

Address-translation scheme for a two-level 32-bit paging architecture is shown in below figure.

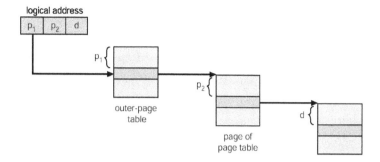

Hashed Page Table:

A common approach for handling address spaces larger than 32 bits is to use a hashed page table, with the hash value being the virtual page number. Each entry in the hash table contains a linked list of elements that has to the same location. Each element consists of three fields: (a) the virtual page number, (b) the value of the mapped page frame, and (c) a pointer to the next element in the linked list. The algorithm works as follows: The virtual page number in the virtual address is hashed into the hash table. The virtual page number is compared to field (a) in the first element in the linked list. If there is a match, the corresponding page frame (field (b)) is used to form the desired physical address. If there is no match, subsequent entries in the linked list are searched for a matching virtual page number. The scheme is shown in below figure.

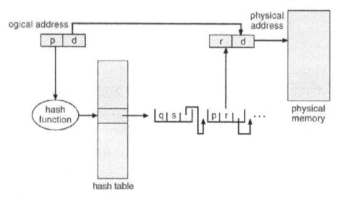

Inverted Page Table

- One entry for each real page (frame) of memory.
- Entry consists of the virtual address of the page stored in that real memory location, with information about the process that owns that page.
- There is only one page table in the system. Not per process.
- Decreases memory needed to store each page table, but increases time needed to search the table when a page reference occurs.
- Use hash table to limit the search to one — or at most a few — page-table entries.

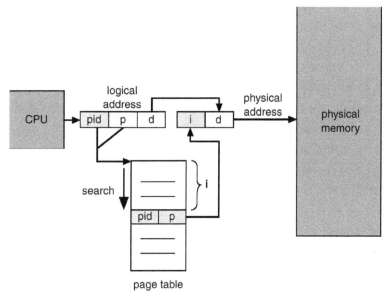

page table

Each virtual address in the system consists of a triple <process-id, page-number, offset>. Each inverted page table entry is a pair <process-id, page-number> where the process-id assumes the role of the address space identifier. When a memory reference occurs, part of the virtual address, consisting of <process-id, page-number>, is presented to the memory subsystem. The inverted page table is then searched for a match. If a match is found say at entry i, then the physical address <i, offset> is generated. If no match is found, then an illegal address access has been attempted.

Shared Page

- Shared code
  - One copy of read-only (reentrant) code shared among processes (i.e., text editors, compilers, window systems).
  - Shared code must appear in same location in the logical address space of all processes.

- Private code and data oEach process keeps a separate copy of the code and data.
  - The pages for the private code and data can appear anywhere in the logical address space.

Reentrant code or pure code is non self modifying code. If the code is reentrant, then it never changes during execution. Thus, two or more processes can execute the same code at the same time. Each process has its own copy of registers and data storage to hold the data for the process' execution. The data for two different processes will of course vary for each process.

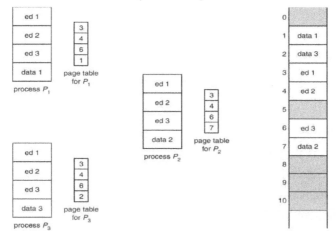

Segmentation

- Memory-management scheme that supports user view of memory.
- A program is a collection of segments. A segment is a logical unit such as:

Main program,
Procedure,
Function,
Method,
Object,
Local variables, global variables,
Common block,
Stack,

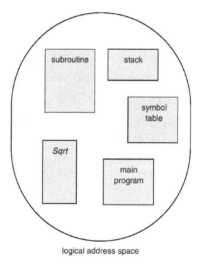

logical address space

Symbol table, arrays

- Segmentation is a memory management scheme that supports this user view of memory.
- A logical address space is a collection of segments. Each segment has a name and a length.

- The addresses specify both the segment name and the offset within the segment.
- The user therefore specifies each address by two quantities such as segment name and an offset. For simplicity of implementation, segments are numbered and are referred to by a segment number, rather than by a segment name.
- Logical address consists of a two tuples:

<segment-number, offset>

- Segment table – maps two-dimensional physical addresses; each table entry has:

  • Base – contains the starting physical address where the segments reside in memory. oLimit – specifies the length of the segment.

- Segment-table base register (STBR) points to the segment table's location in memory.
- Segment-table length register (STLR) indicates number of segments used by a program; Segment number s is legal if s<STLR.

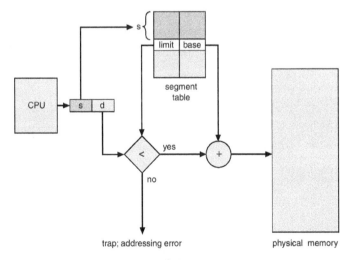

- When the user program is compiled by the compiler it constructs the segments.
- The loader takes all the segments and assigned the segment numbers.
- The mapping between the logical and physical address using the segmentation technique is shown in above figure.
- Each entry in the segment table as limit and base address.
- The base address contains the starting physical address of a segment where the limit address specifies the length of the segment.
- The logical address consists of 2 parts such as segment number and offset.
- The segment number is used as an index into the segment table. Consider the below

example is given below.

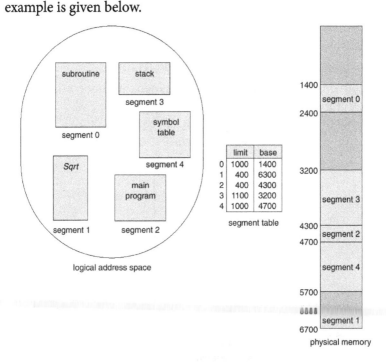

Segmentation with Paging

- Both paging and segmentation have advantages and disadvantages, that's why we can combine these two methods to improve this technique for memory allocation.
- These combinations are best illustrated by architecture of Intel-386.
- The IBM OS/2 is an operating system of the Intel-386 architecture. In this technique both segment table and page table is required.
- The program consists of various segments given by the segment table where the segment table contains different entries one for each segment.
- Then each segment is divided into a number of pages of equal size whose information is maintained in a separate page table.
- If a process has four segments that is 0 to 3 then there will be 4 page tables for that process, one for each segment.
- The size fixed in segmentation table (SMT) gives the total number of pages and therefore maximum page number in that segment with starting from 0.
- If the page table or page map table for a segment has entries for page 0 to 5.
- The address of the entry in the PMT for the desired page p in a given segment s can be obtained by B + P where B can be obtained from the entry in the segmentation table.
- Using the address (B +P) as an index in page map table (page table), the page frame (f) can be obtained and physical address can be obtained by adding offset to page frame.

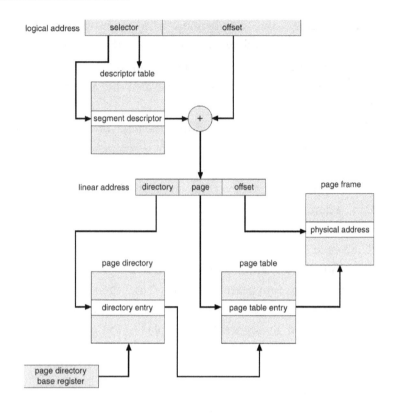

Virtual Memory

- It is a technique which allows execution of process that may not be compiled within the primary memory.
- It separates the user logical memory from the physical memory. This separation allows an extremely large memory to be provided for program when only a small physical memory is available.
- Virtual memory makes the task of programming much easier because the programmer no longer needs to working about the amount of the physical memory is available or not.
- The virtual memory allows files and memory to be shared by different processes by page sharing.
- It is most commonly implemented by demand paging.

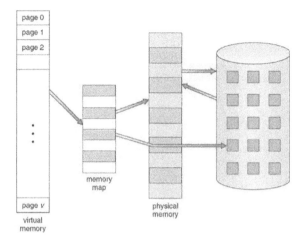

page 0
page 1
page 2
⋮
page v
virtual memory

memory map

physical memory

Demand Paging

A demand paging system is similar to the paging system with swapping feature. When we want to execute a process we swap it into the memory. A swapper manipulates entire process where as a pager is concerned with the individual pages of a process. The demand paging concept is using pager rather than swapper. When a process is to be swapped in, the pager guesses which pages will be used before the process is swapped out again. Instead of swapping in a whole process, the pager brings only those necessary pages into memory. The transfer of a paged memory to contiguous disk space is shown in below figure.

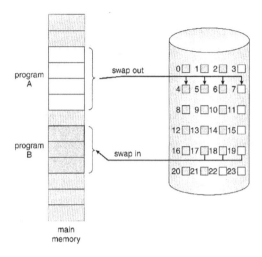

main
memory

Thus it avoids reading into memory pages that will not used any way decreasing the swap time and the amount of physical memory needed. In this technique we need some hardware support to distinct between the pages that are in memory and those that are on the disk. A valid and invalid bit is used for this purpose. When this bit is set to valid it indicates that the associate page is in memory. If the bit is set to invalid it indicates that the page is either not valid or is valid but currently not in the disk.

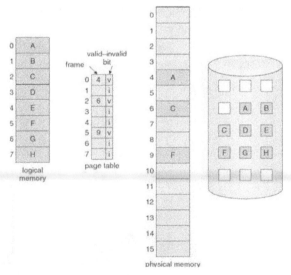

physical memory

Marking a page invalid will have no effect if the process never attempts to access that page. So while a process executes and access pages that are memory resident, execution proceeds normally. Access to a page marked invalid causes a page fault trap. It is the result of the OS's failure to bring the desired page into memory.

Procedure to Handle Page Fault

If a process refers to a page that is not in physical memory then

- We check an internal table (page table) for this process to determine whether the reference was valid or invalid.
- If the reference was invalid, we terminate the process, if it was valid but not yet brought in, we have to bring that from main memory.
- Now we find a free frame in memory.
- Then we read the desired page into the newly allocated frame.
- When the disk read is complete, we modify the internal table to indicate that the page is now in memory.
- We restart the instruction that was interrupted by the illegal address trap. Now the process can access the page as if it had always been in memory.

Page Replacement

- Each process is allocated frames (memory) which hold the process's pages (data)
- Frames are filled with pages as needed – this is called demand paging
- Over-allocation of memory is prevented by modifying the page-fault service routine to replace pages

- The job of the page replacement algorithm is to decide which page gets victimized to make room for a new page
- Page replacement completes separation of logical and physical memory

Page Replacement Algorithm

Optimal Algorithm

- Ideally we want to select an algorithm with the lowest page-fault rate
- Such an algorithm exists, and is called (unsurprisingly) the optimal algorithm:
- Procedure: replace the page that will not be used for the longest time (or at all) – i.e. replace the page with the greatest forward distance in the reference string
- Example using 4 frames:

Reference #	1	2	3	4	5	6	7	8	9	10	11	12
Page referenced	1	2	3	4	1	2	5	1	2	3	4	5
Frames _ = faulting page	1	1	1	1	1	1	1	1	1	1	4	4
		2	2	2	2	2	2	2	2	2	2	2
			3	3	3	3	3	3	3	3	3	3
				4	4	4	5	5	5	5	5	5

- Analysis: 12 page references, 6 page faults, 2 page replacements. Page faults per number of frames = 6/4 = 1.5
- Unfortunately, the optimal algorithm requires special hardware (crystal ball, magic mirror, etc.) not typically found on today's computers
- Optimal algorithm is still used as a metric for judging other page replacement algorithms

FIFO algorithm

- Replaces pages based on their order of arrival: oldest page is replaced
- Example using 4 frames:

Reference #	1	2	3	4	5	6	7	8	9	10	11	12
Page referenced	1	2	3	4	1	2	5	1	2	3	4	5
Frames _ = faulting page	1	1	1	1	1	1	5	5	5	5	4	4
		2	2	2	2	2	2	1	1	1	1	5
			3	3	3	3	3	3	2	2	2	2
				4	4	4	4	4	4	3	3	3

- Analysis: 12 page references, 10 page faults, 6 page replacements. Page faults per number of frames = 10/4 = 2.5

LFU algorithm (page-based)

- Procedure: replace the page which has been referenced least often
- For each page in the reference string, we need to keep a reference count. All reference counts start at 0 and are incremented every time a page is referenced.
- example using 4 frames:

Reference #	1	2	3	4	5	6	7	8	9	10	11	12
Page referenced	1	2	3	4	1	2	5	1	2	3	4	5
Frames _ = faulting page ^{n} = reference count	$^{1}1$	$^{1}1$	$^{1}1$	$^{1}1$	$^{2}1$	$^{2}1$	$^{2}1$	$^{3}1$	$^{3}1$	$^{3}1$	$^{3}1$	$^{3}1$
		$^{1}2$	$^{1}2$	$^{1}2$	$^{1}2$	$^{2}2$	$^{2}2$	$^{2}2$	$^{3}2$	$^{3}2$	$^{3}2$	$^{3}2$
			$^{1}3$	$^{1}3$	$^{1}3$	$^{1}3$	$^{1}5$	$^{1}5$	$^{1}5$	$^{2}3$	$^{2}3$	$^{2}5$
				$^{1}4$	$^{1}4$	$^{1}4$	$^{1}4$	$^{1}4$	$^{1}4$	$^{1}4$	$^{2}4$	$^{2}4$

- At the 7th page in the reference string, we need to select a page to be victimized. Either 3 or 4 will do since they have the same reference count (1). Let's pick 3.
- Likewise at the 10th page reference; pages 4 and 5 have been referenced once each. Let's pick page 4 to victimize. Page 3 is brought in, and its reference count (which was 1 before we paged it out a while ago) is updated to 2.
- Analysis: 12 page references, 7 page faults, 3 page replacements. Page faults per number of frames = 7/4 = 1.75

LFU algorithm (frame-based)

- Procedure: replace the page in the frame which has been referenced least often
- Need to keep a reference count for each frame which is initialized to 1 when the page is paged in, incremented every time the page in the frame is referenced, and reset every time the page in the frame is replaced
- Example using 4 frames:

Reference #	1	2	3	4	5	6	7	8	9	10	11	12
Page referenced	1	2	3	4	1	2	5	1	2	3	4	5
Frames _ = faulting page [n] = reference count	$^{1}1$	$^{1}1$	$^{1}1$	$^{1}1$	$^{2}1$	$^{2}1$	$^{2}1$	$^{3}1$	$^{3}1$	$^{3}1$	$^{3}1$	$^{3}1$
		$^{1}2$	$^{1}2$	$^{1}2$	$^{1}2$	$^{2}2$	$^{2}2$	$^{2}2$	$^{3}2$	$^{3}2$	$^{3}2$	$^{3}2$
			$^{1}3$	$^{1}3$	$^{1}3$	$^{1}3$	$^{1}5$	$^{1}5$	$^{1}5$	$^{1}3$	$^{1}3$	$^{1}5$
				$^{1}4$	$^{1}4$	$^{1}4$	$^{1}4$	$^{1}4$	$^{1}4$	$^{1}4$	$^{2}4$	$^{2}4$

- At the 7th reference, we victimize the page in the frame which has been referenced least often – – in this case, pages 3 and 4 (contained within frames 3 and 4) are candidates, each with a reference count of 1. Let's pick the page in frame 3. Page 5 is paged in and frame 3's reference count is reset to 1.

- At the 10th reference, we again have a page fault. Pages 5 and 4 (contained within frames 3 and 4) are candidates, each with a count of 1. Let's pick page 4. Page 3 is paged into frame 3, and frame 3's reference count is reset to 1.
- Analysis: 12 page references, 7 page faults, 3 page replacements. Page faults per number of frames = 7/4 = 1.75

LRU algorithm

- Replaces pages based on their most recent reference – replace the page with the greatest backward distance in the reference string
- Example using 4 frames:

Reference #	1	2	3	4	5	6	7	8	9	10	11	12
Page referenced	1	2	3	4	1	2	5	1	2	3	4	5
Frames _ = faulting page	1	1	1	1	1	1	1	1	1	1	1	5
		2	2	2	2	2	2	2	2	2	2	2
			3	3	3	3	5	5	5	5	4	4
				4	4	4	4	4	4	3	3	3

- Analysis: 12 page references, 8 page faults, 4 page replacements. Page faults per number of frames = 8/4 = 2
- One possible implementation (not necessarily the best):
  - Every frame has a time field; every time a page is referenced, copy the current time into its frame's time field
  - When a page needs to be replaced, look at the time stamps to find the oldest

Thrashing

- If a process does not have "enough" pages, the page-fault rate is very high

– low CPU utilization
– OS thinks it needs increased multiprogramming
– adds another process to system

- Thrashing is when a process is busy swapping pages in and out
- Thrashing results in severe performance problems. Consider the following scenario, which is based on the actual behaviour of early paging systems. The operating system monitors CPU utilization. If CPU utilization is too low, we increase the degree of multiprogramming by introducing a new process to the system. A global page replacement algorithm is used; it replaces pages with no regard to the process to which they belong. Now suppose that a process enters a new phase in its execution and needs more frames.

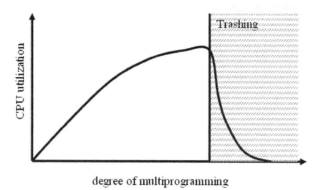

degree of multiprogramming

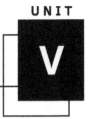
File System

File Concept

A file is a collection of related information that is stored on secondary storage. Information stored in files must be persistent i.e. not affected by power failures & system reboots. Files may be of free from such as text files or may be formatted rigidly. Files represent both programs as well as data.

Part of the OS dealing with the files is known as file system. The important file concepts include:

1. **File attributes:** A file has certain attributes which vary from one operating system to another.

    - ⋏ **Name:** Every file has a name by which it is referred.
    - ⋏ **Identifier:** It is unique number that identifies the file within the file system.
    - ⋏ **Type:** This information is needed for those systems that support different types of files.
    - ⋏ **Location:** It is a pointer to a device & to the location of the file on that device
    - ⋏ **Size:** It is the current size of a file in bytes, words or blocks.
    - ⋏ **Protection:** It is the access control information that determines who can read, write & execute a file.
    - ⋏ **Time, date & user identification:** It gives information about time of creation or last modification & last use.

2. **File operations:** The operating system can provide system calls to create, read, write, reposition, delete and truncate files.

- **Creating files:** Two steps are necessary to create a file. First, space must be found for the file in the file system. Secondly, an entry must be made in the directory for the new file.

- **Reading a file:** Data & read from the file at the current position. The system must keep a read pointer to know the location in the file from where the next read is to take place. Once the read has been taken place, the read pointer is updated.

- **Writing a file:** Data are written to the file at the current position. The system must keep a write pointer to know the location in the file where the next write is to take place. The write pointer must be updated whenever a write occurs.

- **Repositioning within a file (seek):** The directory is searched for the appropriate entry & the current file position is set to a given value. After repositioning data can be read from or written into that position.

- **Deleting a file:** To delete a file, we search the directory for the required file. After deletion, the space is releasedso that it can be reused by other files.

- **Truncating a file:** The user may erase the contents of a file but allows all attributes to remain unchanged expect the file length which is rest to 'O' & the space is released.

3. **File types:** The file name is spilt into 2 parts, Name & extension. Usually these two parts are separated by a period. The user & the OS can know the type of the file from the extension itself.

Listed below are some file types along with their extension:

File Type	Extension
Executable File	exe, bin, com
Object File	obj, o (compiled)
Source Code file	C, C++, Java, pas
Batch File	bat, sh (commands to command the interpreter)
Text File	txt, doc (textual data documents)
Archieve File	arc, zip, tar (related files grouped together into file compressed for storage)
Multimedia File	mpeg (Binary file containing audio or A/V information)

4. **File structure:** Files can be structured in several ways. Three common possible are:

   • **Byte sequence:** The figure shows an unstructured sequence of bytes. The OS doesn't care about the content of file. It only sees the bytes. This structure provides maximum flexibility. Users can write anything into their files & name them according to their convenience. Both UNIX & windows use this approach.

   • **Record sequence:** In this structure, a file is a sequence of fixed length records. Here the read operation returns one records & the write operation overwrites or append or record.

- **Tree:** In this organization, a file consists of a tree of records of varying lengths. Each record consists of a key field. The tree is stored on the key field to allow first searching for a particular key.

Access Methods

Basically, access method is divided into 2 types:

- **Sequential access:** It is the simplest access method. Information in the file is processed in order i.e. one record after another. A process can read all the data in a file in order starting from beginning but can't skip & read arbitrarily from any location. Sequential files can be rewound. It is convenient when storage medium was magnetic tape rather than disk.
- **Direct access:** A file is made up of fixed length-logical records that allow programs to read & write records rapidly in no particular O order. This method can be used when disk are used for storing files. This method is used in many applications e.g. database systems. If an airline customer wants to reserve a seat on a particular flight, the reservation program must be able to access the record for that flight directly without reading the records before it. In a direct access file, there is no restriction in the order of reading or

writing. For example, we can read block 14, then read block 50 & then write block 7 etc. Direct access files are very useful for immediate access to large amount of information.

Directory structure: The file system of computers can be extensive. Some systems store thousands of file on disk. To manage all these data, we need to organize them. The organization is done in 2 steps. The file system is broken into partitions. Each partition contains information about file within it.

Operation on a Directory

- **Search for a file:** We need to be able to search a directory for a particular file.
- **Create a file:** New files are created & added to the directory.
- **Delete a file:** When a file is no longer needed, we may remove it from the directory.
- **List a directory:** We should be able to list the files of the directory.
- **Rename a file:** The name of a file is changed when the contents of the file changes.
- **Traverse the file system:** It is useful to be able to access every directory & every file within a directory.

Structure of a Directory

The most common schemes for defining the structure of the directory are:

1. **Single level directory:** It is the simplest directory structure. All files are present in the same directory. So it is easy to manage & understand.

Limitation: A single level directory is difficult to manage when the no. of files increases or when there is more than one user. Since all files are in same directory, they must have unique names. So, there is confusion of file names between different users.

2. **Two level directories:** The solution to the name collision problem in single level directory is to create a separate directory for each user. In a two level directory structure, each user has its own user file directory. When a user logs in, then master file directory is searched. It is indexed by user name & each entry points to the UFD of that user.

   Limitation: It solves name collision problem. But it isolates one user from another. It is an advantage when users are completely independent. But it is a disadvantage when the users need to access each other's files & co-operate among themselves on a particular task.

3. **Tree structured directories:** It is the most common directory structure. A two level directory is a two level tree. So, the generalization is to extend the directory structure to a tree of arbitrary height. It allows users to create their own subdirectories & organize their files. Every file in the system has a unique path name. It is the path from the root through all the sub-directories to a specified file. A directory is simply another file but it is treated in a special way. One bit in each directory entry defines the entry as a file (O) or as sub – directories. Each user has a current directory. It contains most of the files that are of current interest to the user. Path names can be of two types: An absolute path name begins from the root directory & follows the path down to the specified files. A relative path name defines the path from the current directory. E.g. If the current directory is root/spell/mail, then the relative

path name is prt/first & the absolute path name is root/ spell/ mail/ prt/ first. Here users can access the files of other users also by specifying their path names.

4. **A cyclic graph directory:** It is a generalization of tree structured directory scheme. An a cyclic graph allows directories to have shared sub-directories & files. A shared directory or file is not the same as two copies of a file. Here a programmer can view the copy but the changes made in the file by one programmer are not reflected in the other's copy. But in a shared file, there is only one actual file. So many changes made by a person would be immediately visible to others. This scheme is useful in a situation where several people are working as a team. So, here all the files that are to be shared are put together in one directory. Shared files and sub-directories can be implemented in several ways. A common way used in UNIX systems is to create a new directory entry called link. It is a pointer to another file or sub-directory. The other approach is to duplicate all information in both sharing directories. A cyclic graph structure is more flexible then a tree structure but it is also more complex.

   Limitation: Now a file may have multiple absolute path names. So, distinct file names may refer to the same file. Another problem occurs during deletion of a shared file. When a file is removed by any one user. It may leave dangling pointer to the non existing file. One serious problem in a cyclic graph structure is ensuring that there are no cycles. To avoid these problems, some systems do not allow shared directories or files. E.g. MS-DOS uses a tree structure rather than a cyclic to avoid the problems associated with deletion. One approach for deletion is to preserve the file until all references to it are deleted. To implement this approach, we must have some mechanism for determining the last reference to the file. For this we have to keep a list of reference to a file. But due to the large size of the no. of references. When the count is zero, the file can be deleted.

5. **General graph directory:** When links are added to an existing tree structured directory, the tree structure is destroyed, resulting in a simple graph structure. Linking is a technique that allows a file to appear in more than one directory. The advantage is the simplicity of algorithm to transverse the graph & determines when there are no more references to a file. But a similar problem exists when we are trying to determine when a file can be deleted. Here also a value zero in the reference count means that there are no more references to the file or directory & the file can be deleted. But when cycle exists, the reference count may be non-zero even when there are no references to the directory or file. This occurs due to the possibility of self referencing (cycle) in the structure. So, here we have to use garbage collection scheme to determine when the last references to a file has been deleted & the space can be reallocated. It involves two steps:

- Transverse the entire file system & mark everything that can be accessed.
- Everything that isn't marked is added to the list of free space.

But this process is extremely time consuming. It is only necessary due to presence of cycles in the graph. So, a cyclic graph structure is easier to work than this.

Protection

When information is kept in a computer system, a major concern is its protection from physical damage (reliability) as well as improper access.

Types of access: In case of systems that don't permit access to the files of other users. Protection is not needed. So, one extreme is to provide protection by prohibiting access. The other extreme is to provide free access with no protection. Both these approaches are too extreme for general use. So, we need controlled access. It is provided by limiting the types of file access. Access is permitted depending on several factors. One major factor is type of access requested. The different type of operations that can be controlled are:

- **Read**
- **Write**
- **Execute**
- **Append**
- **Delete**
- **List**

Access Lists and Groups

Various users may need different types of access to a file or directory. So, we can associate an access lists with each file and directory to implement identity dependent access. When a user access requests access to a particular file, the OS checks the access list associated with that file. If that user is granted the requested access, then the access is allowed. Otherwise, a protection violation occurs & the user is denied access to the file. But the main problem with access lists is their length. It is very tedious to construct such a list. So, we use a condensed version of the access list by classifying the users into 3 categories:

- **Owners:** The user who created the file.
- **Group:** A set of users who are sharing the files.
- **Others:** All other users in the system.

Here only 3 fields are required to define protection. Each field is a collection of bits each of which either allows or prevents the access. E.g. The UNIX file system defines 3 fields of 3 bits each: rwx•r(read access)

- w(write access)
- x(execute access)

Separate fields are kept for file owners, group & other users. So, a bit is needed to record protection information for each file.

Allocation Methods

There are 3 methods of allocating disk space widely used.

1. Contiguous allocation

a. It requires each file to occupy a set of contiguous blocks on the disk.

b. Number of disk seeks required for accessing contiguously allocated file is minimum.

c. The IBM VM/CMS OS uses contiguous allocation. Contiguous allocation of a file is defined by the disk address and length (in terms of block units).

d. If the file is 'n' blocks long and starts all location 'b', then it occupies blocks b, b+1, b+2,---------- − − -b+ n-1.

e. The directory for each file indicates the address of the starting block and the length of the area allocated for each file.

f. Contiguous allocation supports both sequential and direct access. For sequential access, the file system remembers the disk address of the last block referenced and reads the next block when necessary.

g. For direct access to block i of a file that starts at block b we can immediately access block b + i.

h. **Problems:** One difficulty with contiguous allocation is finding space for a new file. It also suffers from the problem of external fragmentation. As files are deleted and allocated, the free disk space is broken into small pieces. A major problem in contiguous allocation is how much space is needed for a file. When a file is created, the total amount of space it will need must be found and allocated. Even if the total amount of space needed for a file is known in advances, pre-allocation is inefficient. Because a file that grows very slowly must be allocated enough space for its final size even though most of that space is left unused for a long period time. Therefore, the file has a large amount of internal fragmentation.

2. Linked Allocation

i. Linked allocation solves all problems of contiguous allocation.

j. In linked allocation, each file is linked list of disk blocks, which are scattered throughout the disk.

k. The directory contains a pointer to the first and last blocks of the file.

l. Each block contains a pointer to the next block.

m. These pointers are not accessible to the user. To create a new file, we simply create a new entry in the directory.

n. For writing to the file, a free block is found by the free space management system and this new block is written to & linked to the end of the file.

o. To read a file, we read blocks by following the pointers from block to block.

p. There is no external fragmentation with linked allocation & any free block can be used to satisfy a request.

q. Also there is no need to declare the size of a file when that file is created. A file can continue to grow as long as there are free blocks.

r. **Limitations:** It can be used effectively only for sequential access files. To find the ' i ' th block of the file, we must start at the beginning of that file and follow the pointers until we get the ith block. So it is inefficient to support direct access files. Due to the presence of pointers each file requires slightly more space than before. Another problem is reliability. Since the files are linked together by pointers scattered throughout the disk. What would happen if a pointer were lost or damaged.

3. Indexed Allocation

a. Indexed allocation solves the problem of linked allocation by bringing all the pointers together to one location known as the index block.

b. Each file has its own index block which is an array of disk block addresses. The ith entry in the index block points to the ith block of the file.

c. The directory contains the address of the index block. The read the ith block, we use the pointer in the ith index block entry and read the desired block.

d. To write into the ith block, a free block is obtained from the free space manager and its address is put in the ith index block entry.

e. Indexed allocation supports direct access without suffering external fragmentation.

f. **Limitations:** The pointer overhead of index block is greater than the pointer overhead of linked allocation. So here more space is wasted than linked allocation. In indexed allocation, an entire index block must be allocated, even if most of the pointers are nil.

Free Space Management

Since there is only a limited amount of disk space, it is necessary to reuse the space from the deleted files. To keep track of free disk space, the system maintains a free space list. It records all the disk blocks that are free i.e. not allocated to some file or dictionary. To create a file, we search the free space list for the required amount of space and allocate it to the new file. This space is then removed from the free space list. When a file is deleted, its disk space is added to the free space list.

Implementation

There are 4 ways to implement the free space list such as:

- **Bit Vector:** The free space list is implemented as a bit map or bit vector. Each block is represented as 1 bit. If the block is free, the bit is 1 and if it is allocated then the bit is 0. For example, consider a disk where blocks 2, 3, 4, 5, 8, 9, 10, 11, 12, 13, 17, 18, 25, 26 & 27 are free and rest of the blocks are allocated. The free space bit map would be

  00111100111111000110000000111……………………..

  The main advantage of this approach is that it is simple and efficient to find the first free block or n consecutive free blocks on the disk. But bit vectors are inefficient unless the entire vector is kept in main memory. It is possible for smaller disks but not for larger ones.

- **Linked List:** Another approach is to link together all the free disk blocks and keep a pointer to the first free block. The first free block contains a pointer to the next free block and so on. For example, we keep a pointer to block 2 as the free block. Block 2 contains a pointer to block which points to block 4 which then points to block 5 and so on. But this scheme is not efficient.

  To traverse the list, we must read each block which require a lot of I/O time.

- **Grouping:** In this approach, we store the address of n free blocks in the first free block. The first n-1 of these blocks is actually free. The last block contains the address of another n free blocks and so on. Here the addresses of a large number of free blocks can be found out quickly.

- **Counting:** Rather than keeping a list of n free disk block addresses, we can keep the address of the first free block and the number of free contiguous blocks. So here each entry in the free space list consists of a disk address and a count.

RAID (Redundant Arrays of Independent Disks)

RAID, or "Redundant Arrays of Independent Disks" is a technique which makes use of a combination of multiple disks instead of using a single disk for increased performance, data redundancy or both. The term was coined by David Patterson, Garth A. Gibson, and Randy Katz at the University of California, Berkeley in 1987.

Why data redundancy?

Data redundancy, although taking up extra space, adds to disk reliability. This means, in case of disk failure, if the same data is also backed up onto another disk, we can retrieve the data and go on with the operation. On the other hand, if the data is spread across just multiple disks without the RAID technique, the loss of a single disk can affect the entire data.

Key evaluation points for a RAID System

- **Reliability:** How many disk faults can the system tolerate?
- **Availability:** What fraction of the total session time is a system in uptime mode, i.e. how available is the system for actual use?
- **Performance:** How good is the response time? How high is the throughput (rate of processing work)? Note that performance contains a lot of parameters and not just the two.
- **Capacity:** Given a set of N disks each with B blocks, how much useful capacity is available to the user?

RAID is very transparent to the underlying system. This means, to the host system, it appears as a single big disk presenting itself as a linear array of blocks. This allows older technologies to be replaced by RAID without making too many changes in the existing code.

Different RAID levels

RAID-0 (Striping)

Requiring a minimum of two disks, RAID 0 splits files and stripes the data across two disks or more, treating the striped disks as a single partition. Because multiple hard drives are reading and writing parts of the same file at the same time, throughput is generally faster.RAID 0 does not provide redundancy or fault tolerance. Since it treats multiple disks as a single partition, if even one drive fails, the striped file is unreadable. This is not an insurmountable problem in video streaming or computer gaming environments where performance matters the most, and the source file will still exist even if the stream fails. It is a problem in high availability environments.

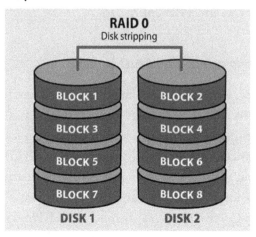

RAID 1: Mirroring

RAID 1 requires a minimum of two disks to work, and provides data redundancy and failover. It reads and writes the exact same data to each disk. Should a mirrored disk fail, the file exists in its entirety on the functioning disk. Once IT replaces the failed desk, the RAID system will automatically mirror back to the replacement drive. RAID 1 also increases read performance.It does take up more usable capacity on drives, but is an economical failover process on application servers.

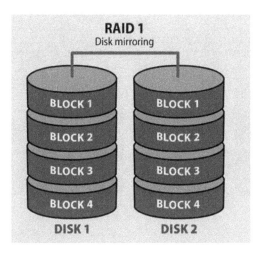

Raid 5: Striping with Parity

This RAID level distributes striping and parity at a block level. Parity is raw binary data. The RAID system calculates its values to create a parity block, which the system uses to recover striped data from a failed drive. Most RAID systems with parity functions store parity blocks on the disks in the array. (Some RAID systems dedicate a disk to parity calculations, but these are rare.)RAID 5 stores parity blocks on striped disks. Each stripe has its own dedicated parity block. RAID 5 can withstand the loss of one disk in the array.RAID 5 combines the performance of RAID 0 with the redundancy of RAID 1, but takes up a lot of storage space to do it – about one third of usable capacity. This level increases write performance since all drives in the array simultaneously serve write requests. However, overall disk performance can suffer from write amplification, since even minor changes to the stripes require multiple steps and recalculations.

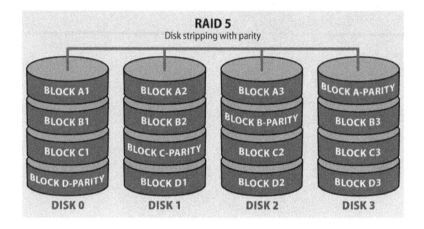

RAID 6: Striping with double parity

This RAID level operates like RAID 5 with distributed parity and striping. The main operational difference in RAID 6 is that there is a minimum of four disks in a RAID 6 array, and the system stores an additional parity block on each desk. This enables a configuration where two disks may fail before the array is unavailable. Its primary usage case or application servers and large storage arrays. RAID 6 offers higher redundancy than 5 and increased read performance. It can suffer from the same server performance overhead with intensive write operations. This performance hit depends on the RAID system architecture: hardware or software, if it's located in firmware, and if the system includes processing software for high-performance parity calculations.

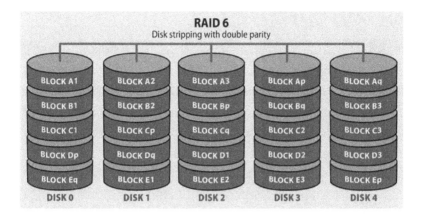

RAID 10: Striping and Mirroring

RAID 10 requires a minimum of four disks in the array. It stripes across disks for higher performance, and mirrors for redundancy. In a four-drive array, the system stripes data to two of the disks. The remaining two disks mirror the striped disks, each one storing half of the data. This RAID level serves environments that require both high data security and high performance, such as high transactional databases that store sensitive information. It is the most expensive of the RAID levels with lower usable capacity and high system costs.

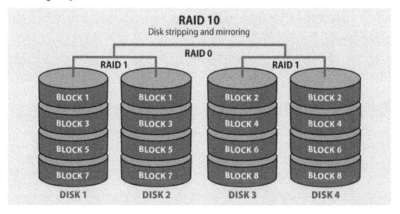

Other RAID Types

- **RAID 2** is an original RAID level but is rarely used today. It is a striping technology that stripes at the bit level instead of the block level, and uses a complex type of error correcting code that takes the place of parity. Raid 2 is generally limited to serving single requests, and its error correction code is far more complex than parity technology.

- **RAID 3** is rarely implemented. It uses byte-level striping and parity, and stores parity calculations on dedicated disk. Like RAID 2, it typically cannot service multiple requests at the same time. This does not affect the performance of large sequential reads and writes, but does slow down random access workloads.

- **RAID 4** stripes block level data and like RAID 5, dedicates a disk to parity. The striping provides high performance for random reads. But because RAID 4 needs to write all parity data to one disk, random write performance suffers.

When researching which RAID level to use, remember that even the best RAID solution cannot take the place of backup. RAID protects data availability and redundancy, but does not recognize or remediate file corruption, write errors, or hacking. IT must always backup and store data on a separate system, ideally a remote one.

I/O Systems

I/O Hardware

I/O-device technology exhibits two conflicting trends. On the one hand, we see increasing standardization of software and hardware interfaces. This trend helps us to incorporate improved device generations into existing computers and operating systems. On the other hand, we see an increasingly broad variety of I/O devices. Some new devices are so unlike previous devices that it is a challenge to incorporate them into our computers and operating systems. This challenge is met by a combination of hardware and software techniques. The basic I/O hardware elements, such as ports, buses, and device controllers, accommodate a wide variety of I/O devices. To encapsulate the details and oddities of different devices, the kernel of an operating system is structured to use device-driver modules. The device drivers present a uniform device access interface to the I/O subsystem, much as system calls provide a standard interface between the application and the operating system.

A device communicates with a computer system by sending signals over a cable or even through the air. The device communicates with the machine via a connection point, or port—for example, a serial port. If devices share a common set of wires, the connection is called a bus. A bus is a set of wires and a rigidly defined protocol that specifies a set of messages that can be sent on the wires. In terms of the electronics, the messages are conveyed by patterns of electrical voltages applied to the wires with defined timings. When device A has a cable that plugs into device B, and device B has a cable that plugs into device C, and device C plugs into a port on the computer, this arrangement is called a daisy chain. A daisy chain usually operates as a bus. Buses are used widely in computer architecture and vary in their signaling methods, speed, throughput, and connection methods. A typical PC bus structure appears in figure. In the figure, a PCI bus (the common PC system bus) connects the processor–memory subsystem to fast devices, and an expansion bus connects relatively slow devices, such as the keyboard and serial and USB ports. In the upper-right portion of the figure, four disks are connected together on a Small Computer System Interface (SCSI) bus plugged into a SCSI controller. Other common buses used to interconnect main parts of a computer include PCI Express (PCIe), with throughput of up to 16 GB per second, and Hyper Transport, with throughput of up to 25 GB per second. A controller is a collection of electronics that can operate a port, a bus, or a device. A serial-port controller is a simple device controller. It is a single chip (or portion of a chip) in the computer that controls the signals on the wires of a serial port. By contrast, a SCSI bus controller is not simple. Because the SCSI protocol is complex, the SCSI bus controller is often implemented as a separate circuit board (or a host adapter) that plugs into the computer. It typically contains a processor, microcode, and some private memory to enable it to process the SCSI protocol messages. Some devices have their own built-in controllers. If you look at a disk drive, you will see a circuit board attached to one side. This board is the disk controller. It implements the disk side of the protocol for some kind of connection—SCSI or Serial Advanced Technology Attachment (SATA), for instance. It has microcode and a processor to do many tasks, such as bad-sector mapping, pre-fetching, buffering, and caching.

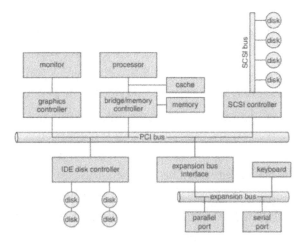

An I/O port typically consists of four registers, called the status, control, data-in, and data-out registers.

- The data-in register is read by the host to get input.
- The data-out register is written by the host to send output.
- The status register contains bits that can be read by the host. These bits indicate states, such as whether the current command has completed, whether a byte is available to be read from the data-in register, and whether a device error has occurred.
- The control register can be written by the host to start a command or to change the mode of a device. For instance, a certain bit in the control register of a serial port chooses between full-duplex and half-duplex communication, another bit enables parity checking, a third bit sets the word length to 7 or 8 bits, and other bits select one of the speeds supported by the serial port.

Polling

The complete protocol for interaction between the host and a controller can be intricate, but the basic handshaking notion is simple. We explain handshaking with an example. Assume that 2 bits are used to coordinate the producer–consumer relationship between the controller and the host. The controller indicates its state through the busy bit in the status register. (Recall that to set a bit means to write a 1 into the bit and to clear a bit means to write a 0 into it.) The controller sets the busy bit when it is busy working and clears the busy bit when it is ready to accept the next command. The host signals its wishes via the command-ready bit in the command register. The host sets the command-ready bit when a command is available for the controller to execute. For this example, the host writes output through a port, coordinating with the controller by handshaking as follows.

1. The host repeatedly reads the busy bit until that bit becomes clear.
2. The host sets the write bit in the command register and writes a byte into the data-out register.
3. The host sets the command-ready bit.
4. When the controller notices that the command-ready bit is set, it sets the busy bit.
5. The controller reads the command register and sees the write command. It reads the data-out register to get the byte and does the I/O to the device.
6. The controller clears the command-ready bit, clears the error bit in the status register to indicate that the device I/O succeeded, and clears the busy bit to indicate that it is finished.

This loop is repeated for each byte. In step 1, the host is busy-waiting or polling: it is in a loop, reading the status register over and over until the busy bit becomes clear. If the controller and device are fast, this method is a reasonable one. But if the wait may be long, the host should probably switch to another task.

How, then, does the host know when the controller has become idle? For some devices, the host must service the device quickly, or data will be lost. For instance, when data are streaming in on a serial port or from a keyboard, the small buffer on the controller will overflow and data will be lost if the host waits too long before returning to read the bytes.

Interrupts

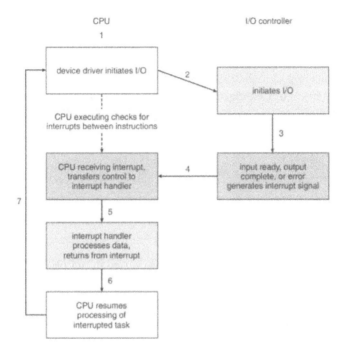

The basic interrupt mechanism works as follows. The CPU hardware has a wire called the interrupt-request line that the CPU senses after executing every instruction. When the CPU detects that a controller has asserted a signal on the interrupt-request line, the CPU performs a state save and jumps to the interrupt-handler routine at a fixed address in memory. The interrupt handler determines the cause of the interrupt, performs the necessary processing, performs a state restore, and executes a return from interrupt instruction to return the CPU to the execution state prior to the interrupt. We say that the device controller raises an interrupt by asserting a signal on the interrupt request line, the CPU catches the interrupt and dispatches it to the interrupt handler, and the handler clears the interrupt by servicing the device. Figure summarizes the interrupt-driven I/O cycle. We stress interrupt management in this chapter because even single-user modern systems manage hundreds of interrupts per second and servers hundreds of thousands per second.

In modern computer hardware, these three features are provided by the CPU and by the interrupt-controller hardware. Most CPUs have two interrupt request lines. One is the nonmaskable interrupt, which is reserved for events such as unrecoverable memory errors. The second interrupt line is maskable: it can be turned off by the CPU before the execution of critical instruction sequences that must not be interrupted. The maskable interrupt is used by device controllers to request service. The interrupt mechanism accepts an address—a number that selects a specific interrupt-handling routine from a small set. In most architectures, this address is an offset in a table called the interrupt vector. This vector contains the memory addresses of specialized interrupt handlers. The purpose of a vectored interrupt mechanism is to reduce the need for a single interrupt handler to search all possible sources of interrupts to determine which one needs service. In practice, however, computers have more devices (and, hence, interrupt handlers) than they have address elements in the interrupt vector. A common way to solve this problem is to use interrupt chaining, in which each element in the interrupt vector points to the head of a list of interrupt handlers. When an interrupt is raised, the handlers on the corresponding list are called one by one, until one is found that can service the request. This structure is a compromise between the overhead of a huge interrupt table and the inefficiency of dispatching to a single interrupt handler. Figure illustrates the design of the interrupt vector for the Intel Pentium processor. The events from 0 to 31, which are nonmaskable, are used to signal various error conditions. The events from 32 to 255, which are maskable, are used for purposes such as device-generated interrupts. The interrupt mechanism also implements a system of interrupt priority levels. These levels enable the CPU to defer the handling of low-priority interrupts without masking all interrupts and makes it possible for a highpriority interrupt to preempt the execution of a low-priority interrupt.

Application I/O Interface

In this section, we discuss structuring techniques and interfaces for the operating system that enable I/O devices to be treated in a standard, uniform way. We explain, for instance, how an application can open a file on a disk without knowing what kind of disk it is and how new disks and other devices can be added to a computer without disruption of the operating system. Like other complex software-engineering problems, the approach here involves abstraction, encapsulation, and software layering Specifically, we can abstract away the detailed differences in I/O devices by identifying a few general kinds. Each general kind is accessed through a standardized set of functions—an interface. The differences are encapsulated in kernel modules called device drivers that internally are custom-tailored to specific devices but that export one of the standard interfaces. Figure illustrates how the I/O-related portions of the kernel are structured in software layers. The purpose of the device-driver layer is to hide the differences among device controllers from the I/O subsystem of the kernel, much as the I/O system calls encapsulate the behavior of devices in a few generic classes that hide hardware differences from applications. Making the I/O subsystem.

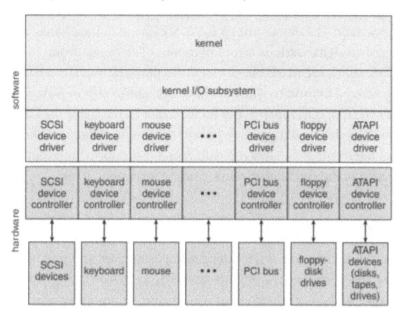

As illustrated in figure

- Character-stream or block. A character-stream device transfers bytes one by one, whereas a block device transfers a block of bytes as a unit.
- Sequential or random access. A sequential device transfers data in a fixed order determined by the device, whereas the user of a random-access device can instruct the device to seek to any of the available data storage locations.
- Synchronous or asynchronous. A synchronous device performs data transfers with predictable response times, in coordination with other aspects of the system. An asynchronous device exhibits irregular or unpredictable response times not coordinated with other computer events.

- Sharable or dedicated. A sharable device can be used concurrently by several processes or threads; a dedicated device cannot.
- Speed of operation. Device speeds range from a few bytes per second to a few gigabytes per second.
- Read–write, read only, or write only. Some devices perform both input and output, but others support only one data transfer direction.

Kernel I/O Subsystem

Kernels provide many services related to I/O. Several services—scheduling, buffering, caching, spooling, device reservation, and error handling—are provided by the kernel's I/O subsystem and build on the hardware and devicedriver infrastructure. The I/O subsystem is also responsible for protecting itself from errant processes and malicious users. I/O Scheduling To schedule a set of I/O requests means to determine a good order in which to execute them. The order in which applications issue system calls rarely is the best choice. Scheduling can improve overall system performance, can share device access fairly among processes, and can reduce the average waiting time for I/O to complete. Here is a simple example to illustrate. Suppose that a disk arm is near the beginning of a disk and that three applications issue blocking read calls to that disk. Application 1 requests a block near the end of the disk, application 2 requests one near the beginning, and application 3 requests one in the middle of the disk. The operating system can reduce the distance that the disk arm travels by serving the applications in the order 2, 3, 1. Rearranging the order of service in this way is the essence of I/O scheduling. Operating-system developers implement scheduling by maintaining a wait queue of requests for each device. When an application issues a blocking I/O system call, the request is placed on the queue for that device. The I/O scheduler rearranges the order of the queue to improve the overall system efficiency and the average response time experienced by applications. The operating system may also try to be fair, so that no one application receives especially poor service, or it may give priority service for delay-sensitive requests. For instance, requests from the virtual memory subsystem may take priority over application requests. Several scheduling algorithms for disk I/O are detailed in Section 10.4. When a kernel supports asynchronous I/O, it must be able to keep track of many I/O requests at the same time. For this purpose, the operating system might attach the wait queue to a device-status table. The kernel manages this table, which contains an entry for each I/O device, as shown in figure

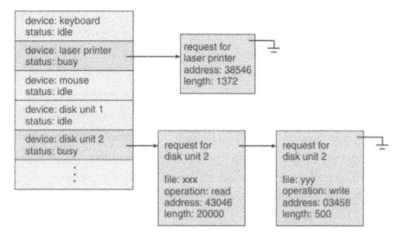

Each table entry indicates the device's type, address, and state (not functioning, idle, or busy). If the device is busy with a request, the type of request and other parameters will be stored in the table entry for that device. Scheduling I/O operations is one way in which the I/O subsystem improves the efficiency of the computer. Another way is by using storage space in main memory or on disk via buffering, caching, and spooling.

Buffering

A buffer, of course, is a memory area that stores data being transferred between two devices or between a device and an application. Buffering is done for three reasons. One reason is to cope with a speed mismatch between the producer and consumer of a data stream. Suppose, for example, that a file is being received via modem for storage on the hard disk. The modem is about a thousand times slower than the hard disk. So a buffer is created in main memory to accumulate the bytes received from the modem. When an entire buffer of data has arrived, the buffer can be written to disk in a single operation. Since the disk write is not instantaneous and the modem still needs a place to store additional incoming data, two buffers are used. After the modem fills the first buffer, the disk write is requested. The modem then starts to fill the second buffer while the first buffer is written to disk. By the time the modem has filled the second buffer, the disk write from the first one should have completed, so the modem can switch back to the first buffer while the disk writes the second one. This double buffering decouples the producer of data from the consumer, thus relaxing timing requirements between them. The need for this decoupling is illustrated in figure, which lists the enormous differences in device speeds for typical computer hardware. A second use of buffering is to provide adaptations for devices that have different data-transfer sizes. Such disparities are especially common in computer networking, where buffers are used widely for fragmentation and reassembly of messages. At the sending side, a large message is fragmented into small network packets. The packets are sent over the network, and the receiving side places them in a reassembly buffer to form an image of the source data. A third use of buffering is to support copy semantics for application I/O. An example will clarify the meaning of "copy semantics." Suppose that an application has a buffer of data that it wishes to write to disk. It calls the write() system call, providing a pointer to the buffer and an integer specifying the number of bytes to write. After the system call returns, what happens if the application changes the contents of the buffer? With copy semantics, the version of the data written to disk is guaranteed to be the version at the time of the application system call, independent of any subsequent changes in the application's buffer. A simple way in which the operating system can guarantee copy semantics is for the write() system call to copy the application data into a kernel buffer before returning control to the application. The disk write is performed from the kernel buffer, so that subsequent changes to the application buffer have no effect. Copying of data between kernel buffers and application data space is common in operating systems, despite the overhead that this operation introduces, because of the clean semantics. The same effect can be obtained more efficiently by clever use of virtual memory mapping and copy-on-write page protection.

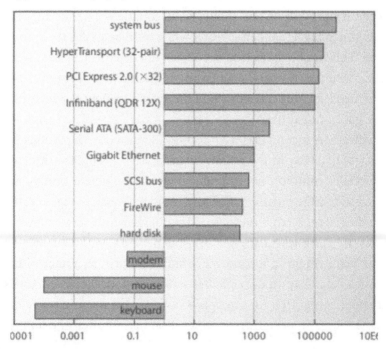

Transforming I/O Requests to Hardware Operations

Earlier, we described the handshaking between a device driver and a device controller, but we did not explain how the operating system connects an application request to a set of network wires or to a specific disk sector. Consider, for example, reading a file from disk. The application refers to the data by a file name. Within a disk, the file system maps from the file name through the file-system directories to obtain the space allocation of the file. For instance, in MS-DOS, the name maps to a number that indicates an entry in the file-access table, and that table entry tells which disk blocks are allocated to the file. In UNIX, the name maps to an inode number, and the corresponding inode contains the space-allocation information. But how is the connection made from the file name to the disk controller (the hardware port address or the memory-mapped controller registers)? One method is that used by MS-DOS, a relatively simple operating system. The first part of an MS-DOS file name, preceding the colon, is a string that identifies a specific hardware device. For example, C: is the first part of every file name on the primary hard disk. The fact that C: represents the primary hard disk is built into the operating system; C: is mapped to a specific port address through a device table. Because of the colon separator, the device name space is separate from the file-system name space. This separation makes it easy for the operating system to associate extra functionality with each device. For instance, it is easy to invoke spooling on any files written to the printer. If, instead, the device name space is incorporated in the regular file-system name space, as it is in UNIX, the normal file-system name services are provided automatically. If the file system provides ownership and access control to all file names, then devices have owners and access control. Since files are stored on devices, such an interface provides access to the I/O system at two levels. Names can be used to access the devices themselves or to access the files stored on the devices. UNIX represents device names in the regular file-system name space. Unlike an MS-DOS file name, which has a colon separator, a UNIX path name has no clear separation of the device portion. In fact, no part of the path name is the name of a device. UNIX has a mount table that associates prefixes of path names with specific device names. To resolve a path name, UNIX looks up the name in the mount table to find the longest matching prefix; the corresponding entry in the mount table gives the device name. This device name also has the form of a name in the file-system name space. When UNIX looks up this name in the file-system directory structures, it finds not an inode number but a device number. The major device number identifies a device driver that should be called to handle I/O to this device. The minor device number is passed to the device driver to index into a device table. The corresponding device-table entry gives the port address or the memory-mapped address of the device controller. Modern operating systems gain significant flexibility from the multiple stages of lookup tables in the path between a request and a physical device controller. The mechanisms that pass requests between applications and drivers are general. Thus, we can introduce new devices and drivers into a computer without recompiling the kernel. In fact, some operating systems have the ability to load device drivers on demand. At boot time, the system first probes the hardware buses to determine what devices are present. It then loads in the necessary drivers, either immediately or when first required by an I/O request. We next describe the typical life cycle of a blocking read request, as depicted in figure. The figure suggests that an I/O operation requires a great many steps that together consume a tremendous number of CPU cycles.

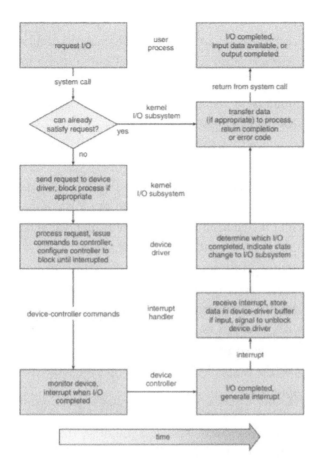

1. A process issues a blocking read() system call to a file descriptor of a file that has been opened previously.
2. The system-call code in the kernel checks the parameters for correctness. In the case of input, if the data are already available in the buffer cache, the data are returned to the process, and the I/O request is completed.
3. Otherwise, a physical I/O must be performed. The process is removed from the run queue and is placed on the wait queue for the device, and the I/O request is scheduled. Eventually, the I/O subsystem sends the request to the

device driver. Depending on the operating system, the request is sent via a subroutine call or an in-kernel message.

4. The device driver allocates kernel buffer space to receive the data and schedules the I/O. Eventually, the driver sends commands to the device controller by writing into the device-control registers.

5. The device controller operates the device hardware to perform the data transfer.

6. The driver may poll for status and data, or it may have set up a DMA transfer into kernel memory. We assume that the transfer is managed by a DMA controller, which generates an interrupt when the transfer completes.

7. The correct interrupt handler receives the interrupt via the interrupt vector table, stores any necessary data, signals the device driver, and returns from the interrupt.

8. The device driver receives the signal, determines which I/O request has completed, determines the request's status, and signals the kernel I/O subsystem that the request has been completed.

9. The kernel transfers data or return codes to the address space of the requesting process and moves the process from the wait queue back to the ready queue.

10. Moving the process to the ready queue unblocks the process. When the scheduler assigns the process to the CPU, the process resumes execution at the completion of the system call.

Streams

UNIX System V has an interesting mechanism, called STREAMS, that enables an application to assemble pipelines of driver code dynamically. A stream is a full-duplex connection between a device driver and a user-level process. It consists of a stream head that interfaces with the user process, a driver end that controls the device, and zero or more stream modules between the stream head and the driver end. Each of these components contains a pair of queues —a read queue and a write queue. Message passing is used to transfer data between queues. The STREAMS structure is shown in figure. Modules provide the functionality of STREAMS processing; they are pushed onto a stream by use of the ioctl() system call. For example, a process can open a serial-port device via a stream and can push on a module to handle input editing. Because messages are exchanged between queues in adjacent modules, a queue in one module may overflow an adjacent queue. To prevent this from occurring, a queue may support flow control. Without flow control, a queue accepts all messages and immediately sends them on to the queue in the adjacent module without buffering them. A queue that supports flow control buffers messages and does not accept messages without sufficient buffer space. This process involves exchanges of control messages between queues in adjacent modules. A user process writes data to a device using either the write() or putmsg() system call. The write() system call writes raw data to the stream, whereas putmsg() allows the user process to specify a message. Regardless of the system call used by the user process, the stream head copies the data into a message and delivers it to the queue for the next module in line. This copying of messages continues until the message is copied to the driver end and hence the device. Similarly, the user process reads data from the stream head using either the read() or getmsg() system call. If read() is used, the stream head gets a message from its adjacent queue and returns ordinary data (an unstructured byte stream) to the process. If getmsg() is used, a message is returned to the process.

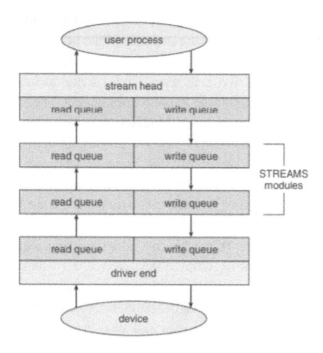

STREAMS I/O is asynchronous (or nonblocking) except when the user process communicates with the stream head. When writing to the stream, the user process will block, assuming the next queue uses flow control, until there is room to copy the message. Likewise, the user process will block when reading from the stream until data are available. As mentioned, the driver end—like the stream head and modules—has a read and write queue. However, the driver end must respond to interrupts, such as one triggered when a frame is ready to be read from a network. Unlike the stream head, which may block if it is unable to copy a message to the next queue in line, the driver end must handle all incoming data. Drivers must support flow control as well. However, if a device's buffer is full, the device typically resorts to dropping incoming messages. Consider a network card whose input buffer is full. The network card must simply drop further messages until there is enough buffer space to store incoming messages. The benefit of using STREAMS is that it provides a framework for a modular and incremental approach to writing device drivers and network protocols. Modules may be used by different streams and hence by different devices. For example, a networking module may be used by both an Ethernet network card and a 802.11 wireless network card. Furthermore, rather than treating character-device I/O as an unstructured byte stream, STREAMS allows support for message boundaries and control information when communicating between modules. Most UNIX variants support STREAMS, and it is the preferred method for writing protocols and device drivers. For example, System V UNIX and Solaris implement the socket mechanism using STREAMS.

Performance

I/O is a major factor in system performance. It places heavy demands on the CPU to execute device-driver code and to schedule processes fairly and efficiently as they block and unblock. The resulting context switches stress the CPU and its hardware caches. I/O also exposes any inefficiencies in the interrupt-handling mechanisms in the kernel. In addition, I/O loads down the memory bus during data copies between controllers and physical memory and again during copies between kernel buffers and application data space. Coping gracefully with all these demands is one of the major concerns of a computer architect. Although modern computers can handle many thousands of interrupts per second, interrupt handling is a relatively expensive task. Each interrupt causes the system to perform a state change, to execute the interrupt handler, and then to restore state. Programmed I/O can be more efficient than interrupt-driven I/O, if the number of cycles spent in busy waiting is not excessive. An I/O completion typically unblocks a process, leading to the full overhead of a context switch. Network traffic can also cause a high context-switch rate. Consider, for instance, a remote login from one machine to another. Each character typed on the local machine must be transported to the remote machine. On the local machine, the character is typed; a keyboard interrupt is generated; and the character is passed through the interrupt handler to the device driver, to the kernel, and then to the user process. The user process issues a network I/O system call to send the character to the remote machine. The character then flows into the local kernel, through the network layers that construct a network packet, and into the network device driver. The network device driver transfers the packet to the network controller, which sends the character and generates an interrupt. The interrupt is passed back up through the kernel to cause the network I/O system call to complete.

Goals of Protection

Obviously to prevent malicious misuse of the system by users or programs. See chapter 15 for a more thorough coverage of this goal. To ensure that each shared resource is used only in accordance with system *policies*, which may be set either by system designers or by system administrators. To ensure that errant programs cause the minimal amount of damage possible. Note that protection systems only provide the *mechanisms* for enforcing policies and ensuring reliable systems. It is up to administrators and users to implement those mechanisms effectively.

Principles of Protection

The **principle of least privilege** dictates that programs, users, and systems be given just enough privileges to perform their tasks. This ensures that failures do the least amount of harm and allow the least of harm to be done. For example, if a program needs special privileges to perform a task, it is better to make it a SGID program with group ownership of "network" or "backup" or some other pseudo group, rather than SUID with root ownership. This limits the amount of damage that can occur if something goes wrong.Typically each user is given their own account, and has only enough privilege to modify their own files.The root account should not be used for normal day to day activities – The System Administrator should also have an ordinary account, and reserve use of the root account for only those tasks which need the root privileges.

Domain of Protection

A computer can be viewed as a collection of *processes* and *objects* (both HW & SW).The **need to know principle** states that a process should only have access to those objects it needs to accomplish its task, and furthermore only in the modes for which it needs access and only during the time frame when it needs access.The modes available for a particular object may depend upon its type.

Domain Structure

A **protection domain** specifies the resources that a process may access Each domain defines a set of objects and the types of operations that may be invoked on each object.An **access right** is the ability to execute an operation on an object.A domain is defined as a set of <object, {access right set }> pairs, as shown below. Note that some domains may be disjoint while others overlap.

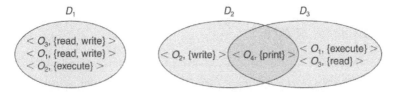

Fig: System with three protection domains.

The association between a process and a domain may be *static* or *dynamic.*

- If the association is static, then the need-to-know principle requires a way of changing the contents of the domain dynamically.
- If the association is dynamic, then there needs to be a mechanism for **domain switching.**

Domains may be realized in different fashions – as users, or as processes, or as procedures. E.g. if each user corresponds to a domain, then that domain defines the access of that user, and changing domains involves changing user ID.

An Example: UNIX

UNIX associates domains with users.Certain programs operate with the SUID bit set, which effectively changes the user ID, and therefore the access domain, while the program is running. (and similarly for the SGID bit.) Unfortunately this has some potential for abuse.An alternative used on some systems is to place privileged programs in special directories, so that they attain the identity of the directory owner when they run. This prevents crackers from placing SUID programs in random directories around the system. Yet another alternative is to not allow the changing of ID at all. Instead, special privileged daemons are launched at boot time, and user processes send messages to these daemons when they need special tasks performed.

An Example: MULTICS

The MULTICS system uses a complex system of rings, each corresponding to a different protection domain, as shown below:

Rings are numbered from 0 to 7, with outer rings having a subset of the privileges of the inner rings.Each file is a memory segment, and each segment description includes an entry that indicates the ring number associated with that segment, as well as read, write, and execute privileges.Each process runs in a ring, according to the *current-ring-number,* a counter associated with each process.A process operating in one ring can only access segments associated with higher (farther out) rings, and then only according to the access bits. Processes cannot access segments associated with lower rings.Domain switching is achieved by a process in one ring calling upon a process operating in a lower ring, which is controlled by several factors stored with each segment descriptor:

- An *access bracket*, defined by integers $b1 <= b2$.
- A *limit* $b3 > b2$
- A *list of gates,* identifying the entry points at which the segments may be called.

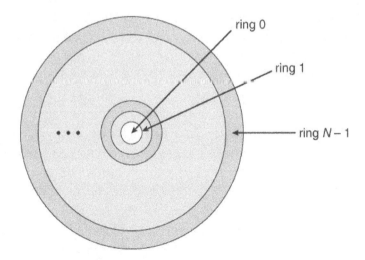

Figure: – MULTICS ring structure.

If a process operating in ring i calls a segment whose bracket is such that b1 <= i<= b2, then the call succeeds and the process remains in ring i.Otherwise a trap to the OS occurs, and is handled as follows:

- If i<b1, then the call is allowed, because we are transferring to a procedure with fewer privileges. However if any of the parameters being passed are of segments below b1, then they must be copied to an area accessible by the called procedure.
- If i> b2, then the call is allowed only if i<= b3 and the call is directed to one of the entries on the list of gates.

Overall this approach is more complex and less efficient than other protection schemes.

Access Matrix

The model of protection that we have been discussing can be viewed as an *access matrix,* in which columns represent different system resources and rows represent different protection domains. Entries within the matrix indicate what access that domain has to that resource.

object domain	F_1	F_2	F_3	printer
D_1	read		read	
D_2				print
D_3		read	execute	
D_4	read write		read write	

Figure – Access matrix.

Domain switching can be easily supported under this model, simply by providing "switch" access to other domains

domain \ object	F_1	F_2	F_3	laser printer	D_1	D_2	D_3	D_4
D_1	read		read			switch		
D_2				print			switch	switch
D_3		read	execute					
D_4	read write		read write		switch			

Figure – Access matrix of Figure with domains as objects.

The ability to *copy* rights is denoted by an asterisk, indicating that processes in that domain have the right to copy that access within the same column, i.e. for the same object. There are two important variations:

- If the asterisk is removed from the original access right, then the right is *transferred,* rather than being copied. This may be termed a *transfer* right as opposed to a *copy* right.
- If only the right and not the asterisk is copied, then the access right is added to the new domain, but it may not be propagated further. That is the new domain does not also receive the right to copy the access. This may be termed a *limited copy* right, as shown in Figure below:

object domain	F_1	F_2	F_3
D_1	execute		write*
D_2	execute	read*	execute
D_3	execute		

(a)

object domain	F_1	F_2	F_3
D_1	execute		write*
D_2	execute	read*	execute
D_3	execute	read	

(b)

Figure – Access matrix with *copy* rights.

The *owner* right adds the privilege of adding new rights or removing existing ones:

object \ domain	F_1	F_2	F_3
D_1	owner execute		write
D_2		read* owner	read* owner write
D_3	execute		

(a)

object \ domain	F_1	F_2	F_3
D_1	owner execute		write
D_2		owner read* write*	read* owner write
D_3		write	write

(b)

Figure – Access matrix with *owner* rights.

- Copy and owner rights only allow the modification of rights within a column. The addition of ***control rights***, which only apply to domain objects, allow a process operating in one domain to affect the rights available in other domains. For example in the table below, a process operating in domain D2 has the right to control any of the rights in domain D4.

domain \ object	F_1	F_2	F_3	laser printer	D_1	D_2	D_3	D_4
D_1	read		read			switch		
D_2				print			switch	switch control
D_3		read	execute					
D_4	write		write		switch			

Figure – Modified access matrix

Implementation of Access Matrix

Global Table

The simplest approach is one big global table with <domain, object, rights> entries.Unfortunately this table is very large (even if sparse) and so cannot be kept in memory (without invoking virtual memory techniques.)There is also no good way to specify groupings – If everyone has access to some resource, then it still needs a separate entry for every domain.

Access Lists for Objects

Each column of the table can be kept as a list of the access rights for that particular object, discarding blank entries.For efficiency a separate list of default access rights can also be kept, and checked first.

Capability Lists for Domains

In a similar fashion, each row of the table can be kept as a list of the capabilities of that domain.Capability lists are associated with each domain, but not directly accessible by the domain or any user process.Capability lists are themselves protected resources, distinguished from other data in one of two ways:

- A *tag,* possibly hardware implemented, distinguishing this special type of data. (other types may be floats, pointers, booleans, etc.)
- The address space for a program may be split into multiple segments, at least one of which is inaccessible by the program itself, and used by the operating system for maintaining the process's access right capability list.

Access Control

Role-Based Access Control, RBAC, assigns privileges to users, programs, or roles as appropriate, where "privileges" refer to the right to call certain system calls, or to use certain parameters with those calls.RBAC supports the principle of least privilege, and reduces the susceptibility to abuse as opposed to SUID or SGID programs.

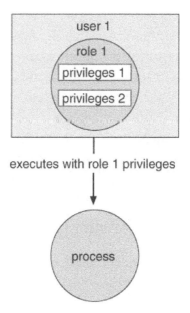

Figure – Role-based access control in Solaris 10.

Revocation of Access Rights

The need to revoke access rights dynamically raises several questions:

- Immediate versus delayed – If delayed, can we determine when the revocation will take place?
- Selective versus general – Does revocation of an access right to an object affect *all* users who have that right, or only some users?
- Partial versus total – Can a subset of rights for an object be revoked, or are all rights revoked at once?
- Temporary versus permanent – If rights are revoked, is there a mechanism for processes to re-acquire some or all of the revoked rights?

With an access list scheme revocation is easy, immediate, and can be selective, general, partial, total, temporary, or permanent, as desired.With capabilities lists the problem is more complicated, because access rights are distributed throughout the system. A few schemes that have been developed include:

- Reacquisition – Capabilities are periodically revoked from each domain, which must then re-acquire them.
- Back-pointers – A list of pointers is maintained from each object to each capability which is held for that object.
- Indirection – Capabilities point to an entry in a global table rather than to the object. Access rights can be revoked by changing or invalidating the table entry, which may affect multiple processes, which must then re-acquire access rights to continue.
- Keys – A unique bit pattern is associated with each capability when created, which can be neither inspected nor modified by the process.

  ▲ A master key is associated with each object.

⋏ When a capability is created, its key is set to the object's master key.

⋏ As long as the capability's key matches the object's key, then the capabilities remain valid.

⋏ The object master key can be changed with the set-key command, thereby invalidating all current capabilities.

⋏ More flexibility can be added to this scheme by implementing a *list* of keys for each object, possibly in a global table.

Security

Security refers to providing a protection system to computer system resources such as CPU, memory, disk, software programs and most importantly data/information stored in the computer system. If a computer program is run by an unauthorized user, then he/she may cause severe damage to computer or data stored in it. So a computer system must be protected against unauthorized access, malicious access to system memory, viruses, worms etc. We're going to discuss following topics in this chapter.

- Authentication
- One Time passwords
- Program Threats
- System Threats
- Computer Security Classifications

Authentication

Authentication refers to identifying each user of the system and associating the executing programs with those users. It is the responsibility of the Operating System to create a protection system which ensures that a user who is running a particular program is authentic. Operating Systems generally identifies/ authenticates users using following three ways –

- **Username / Password** – User need to enter a registered username and password with Operating system to login into the system.
- **User card/key** – User need to punch card in card slot, or enter key generated by key generator in option provided by operating system to login into the system.
- **User attribute – fingerprint/ eye retina pattern/ signature** – User need to pass his/her attribute via designated input device used by operating system to login into the system.

One Time passwords

One-time passwords provide additional security along with normal authentication. In One-Time Password system, a unique password is required every time user tries to login into the system. Once a one-time password is used, then it cannot be used again. One-time password are implemented in various ways.

- **Random numbers** – Users are provided cards having numbers printed along with corresponding alphabets. System asks for numbers corresponding to few alphabets randomly chosen.
- **Secret key** – User are provided a hardware device which can create a secret id mapped with user id. System asks for such secret id which is to be generated every time prior to login.
- **Network password** – Some commercial applications send one-time passwords to user on registered mobile/ email which is required to be entered prior to login.

Program Threats

Operating system's processes and kernel do the designated task as instructed. If a user program made these process do malicious tasks, then it is known as **Program Threats**. One of the common example of program threat is a program installed in a computer which can store and send user credentials via network to some hacker. Following is the list of some well-known program threats.

- **Trojan Horse** – Such program traps user login credentials and stores them to send to malicious user who can later on login to computer and can access system resources.
- **Trap Door** – If a program which is designed to work as required, have a security hole in its code and perform illegal action without knowledge of user then it is called to have a trap door.
- **Logic Bomb** – Logic bomb is a situation when a program misbehaves only when certain conditions met otherwise it works as a genuine program. It is harder to detect.
- **Virus** – Virus as name suggest can replicate themselves on computer system. They are highly dangerous and can modify/delete user files, crash systems. A virus is generatlly a small code embedded in a program. As user accesses the program, the virus starts getting embedded in other files/ programs and can make system unusable for user

System Threats

System threats refers to misuse of system services and network connections to put user in trouble. System threats can be used to launch program threats on a complete network called as program attack. System threats creates such an environment that operating system resources/ user files are misused. Following is the list of some well-known system threats.

- **Worm** – Worm is a process which can choked down a system performance by using system resources to extreme levels. A Worm process generates its multiple copies where each copy uses system resources, prevents all other processes to get required resources. Worms processes can even shut down an entire network.
- **Port Scanning** – Port scanning is a mechanism or means by which a hacker can detects system vulnerabilities to make an attack on the system.
- **Denial of Service** – Denial of service attacks normally prevents user to make legitimate use of the system. For example, a user may not be able to use internet if denial of service attacks browser›s content settings.

User Authentication

User authentication process is used just to identify who the owner is or who the identified person is.In personal computer, generally, user authentication can be perform using password. When a computer user wants to log into a computer system, then the installed operating system (OS) on that computer system generally wants to determine or check who the user is. This process is called as user authentication.Sometime it is too important to authenticate the user because the computer system may have some important documents of the owner.Most methods of authenticating the computer users when they attempt or try to log into the system are based on one of the following three principles:

- Something, the user knowns
- Something, the user has
- Something, the user is

That computer users who want to cause some trouble on any specific computer system, have to first log into that computer systems, means getting past whichever the authentication method or procedure is used. Those computer users are called as hackers.Basically, hacker is a term of honour that is reserved for or given to a great computer programmer as normal computer user or programmer can't get access into anyone's system without permission.User can be authenticated through one of the following way:

- User authentication using password
- User authentication using physical object
- User authentication using biometric
- User authentication using countermeasures

Now let's describe briefly about all the above authentication process one by one.

User Authentication using Password

User authentication using password is the most widely used form of authenticating the user.In this method of authenticating the user with password, it is to require that the user who is going to authenticate has to type their login name or id and login password. Authenticating the user using their password is an easy method and also easy to implement.Keeping a central list of pairs is the simplest implementation of user authentication using password method.Here, in this method, the login name typed in is looked up in the list and typed password is then compared to stored password.Now, if both login and password match, then the login is allowed or the user is successfully authenticated and approved to log into that system. And in case if now match occurred, then the login error is detected.

How to Improve Password Security?

Here are the list of four basic and common way to secure the password:

- Password should be minimum of eight characters
- Password should contain both uppercase and lowercase letters
- Password should contain at least one digit and one special characters
- Don't use dictionary words and known name such as stick, mouth, sun, albert etc.

One Time Password (OTP)

One Time Password (OTP) is the most extreme form of changing the password all the time. One time password is a very safe way to implement. When OTPs are used, the user get a book containing a list of many passwords. Each login uses the next password in the list. Therefore, if an intruder ever discover the password, then it willnot do any good for him as the next time, a different password must be used.

User Authentication using Physical Object

User authentication using a physical object is a second way to authenticate the user here. Here, physical object may refer to Bank's Automated Teller Machine (ATM) card or any other plastic card that is used to authenticate. To authenticate the user, plastic card is inserted by the user into a reader associated with the terminal or computer system. Generally, the user must not only insert the card that is used as physical object to authenticate him/her, but also type in a password just to prevent someone from using a lost or stolen card.

User Authentication using Biometric

User authentication using biometric is the third authentication method here. This method measures the physical characteristics of the user that are very hard to forge. These are called as biometrics. User authentication using biometric's example is a fingerprint, voiceprint, or retina scan reader in the terminal could verify the identity of the user. Basically, the typical biometric system has the following two parts:

- Enrolment
- Identification

Now, let's describe briefly about the above two parts of the biometric system.

Enrolment

In biometric system, during enrolment, characteristics of the user are measured and the results digitized. Then, significant features are extracted and stored in the record associated with the user. The record can be kept or stored in a central or main database or stored on a smart card that the user carrier around and inserts into a remote reader, for example, at an ATM machine.

Identification

In identification, the user shows up and provides a login name or id. Now, again, the system makes the measurement. Now, if the new values match the ones sampled at enrolment time, then the login is accepted, otherwise the login attempt is rejected.

Firewalling to Protect Systems and Networks

We turn next to the question of how a trusted computer can be connected safely to an untrustworthy network. One solution is the use of a firewall to separate trusted and untrusted systems. A firewall is a computer, appliance, or router that sits between the trusted and the untrusted. A network firewall limits network access between the two security domains and monitors and logs all connections. It can also limit connections based on source or destination address, source or destination port, or direction of the connection. For instance, web servers use HTTP to communicate with web browsers. A firewall therefore may allow only HTTP to pass from all hosts outside the firewall to the web server within the firewall. The Morris Internet worm used the finger protocol to break into computers, so finger would not be allowed to pass, for example.

In fact, a network firewall can separate a network into multiple domains. A common implementation has the Internet as the untrusted domain; a semitrusted and semi-secure network, called the demilitarized zone (DMZ), as another domain; and a company's computers as a third domain. Connections are allowed from the Internet to the DMZ computers and from the company computers to the Internet but are not allowed from the Internet or DMZ computers to the company computers. Optionally, controlled communications may be allowed between the DMZ and one company computer or more. For instance, a web server on the DMZ may need to query a database server on the corporate network.

With a firewall, however, access is contained, and any DMZ systems that are broken into still are unable to access the company computers. Of course, a firewall itself must be secure and attack-proof; otherwise, its ability to secure connections can be compromised. Furthermore, firewalls do not prevent attacks that tunnel, or travel within protocols or connections that the firewall allows. A buffer-overflow attack to a web server will not be stopped by the firewall, for example, because the HTTP connection is allowed; it is the contents of the HTTP connection that house the attack. Likewise, denial-ofservice attacks can affect firewalls as much as any other machines. Another vulnerability of firewalls is spoofing, in which an unauthorized host pretends to be an authorized host by meeting some authorization criterion. For example, if a firewall rule allows a connection from a host and identifies that host by its IP address, then another host could send packets using that same address and be allowed through the firewall.

In addition to the most common network firewalls, there are other, newer kinds of firewalls, each with its pros and cons. A personal firewall is a software layer either included with the operating system or added as an application. Rather than limiting communication between security domains, it limits communication to (and possibly from) a given host. A user could add a personal firewall to her PC so that a Trojan horse would be denied access to the network to which the PC is connected. An application proxy firewall understands the protocols that applications speak across the network. For example, SMTP is used for mail transfer. An application proxy accepts a connection just as an SMTP server would and then initiates a connection to the original destination SMTP server. It can monitor the traffic as it forwards the message, watching for and disabling illegal commands, attempts to exploit bugs, and so on.

Some firewalls are designed for one specific protocol. An XML firewall, for example, has the specific purpose of analysing XML traffic and blocking disallowed or malformed XML. System-call firewalls sit between applications and the kernel, monitoring system-call execution. For example, in Solaris 10, the "least privilege" feature implements a list of more than fifty system calls that processes may or may not be allowed to make. A process that does not need to spawn other processes can have that ability taken away, for instance.

www.ingramcontent.com/pod-product-compliance
Lightning Source LLC
Chambersburg PA
CBHW051053050326
40690CB00006B/700